The Prophetic Parish

The Prophetic Parish

A Center for Peace and Justice

Dennis J. Geaney

WINSTON PRESS

The triceps is an old Nordic design symbolizing heavenly power. When we trace the design's perimeter downward and back to the apex, we are reminded of God's power descending to earth, traversing the earth, and returning to God. This book envisions peace and justice concerns as two earthly channels of God's power—two channels through which God, with our cooperation, transforms the earth.

Cover design: Sharon Keegan

Excerpts from *The Jerusalem Bible,* copyright © 1966 by Darton, Longman & Todd Ltd. and Doubleday & Company, Inc. Used by permission of the publisher.

Library of Congress Catalog Card Number: 83-50038

ISBN: 0-86683-807-4

Printed in the United States of America

5 4 3 2 1

Winston Press, Inc.
430 Oak Grove
Minneapolis, Minnesota 55403

In memory of
Dorothy Day

Acknowledgments

While I am indebted to countless people with whom I have interacted in the past half century in developing my pastoral theology and praxis, a few specific acknowledgments are in order. A workshop during the summer of 1982 with Joe Holland of Center of Concern gave me the focus for this book. The writings of John Coleman, S.J., a sociologist of religion, helped me to put my day-to-day parochial experiences into a larger context.

I am especially indebted to the parishioners and staff of St. Victor Parish for their high level of tolerance as I nudged them to look at the gospel through my lens. I am especially grateful to St. Victor's gifted pastor, Father Leo Mahon, who invited me to share and bring to reality his dream of the kingdom. His openness to a variety of theological and pastoral perspectives has been for me a source of creativity.

Cyril A. Reilly of Winston Press exhibited heroic patience with me in shaping the manuscript of a busy parish priest into a readable and coherent text. John O'Brien of the *Chicago Tribune* offered invaluable suggestions. Romaine Jamrozy was always willing to give my typing priority over her household chores.

Contents

Foreword...vii

1. Who Wants a Prophetic Parish?...1
2. The Lost American Dream...12
3. Jesus' Call to a Radical Christianity...22
4. The New American Prophetic Church...31
5. The Parish Comes Alive...40
6. Social Sin: A "New" Category...50
7. Work: A Lost Identity...61
8. An Industrial Neighborhood Organizes...68
9. A Peace and Justice Commission...75
10. Women in a Male Church...83
11. A Place for Dissent in the Church...97
12. Wrestling with Our Own Demons...110
13. The Fire-maker Myth...121

Notes...126

Foreword

Many priests and lay people working as a part of the parish today in the U.S.A. will resonate with Father Geaney's account. Somehow he seems to have captured the spirit of what problems and challenges face a parish that is alive; he describes so well the growing pains and joys which go with involvement. His is not the view of a freshly ordained curate, but the weighed experiences of a seasoned follower of the Gospel.

Some may not always agree with the solutions Father Geaney suggests; some may even feel he goes too far; but he does not hesitate to say it as he sees it, and for that we can all be grateful.

Some years ago many were saying that the parish as we know it would be dead before a decade went by. Time is showing this is not true. The parish is still very much alive and probably stronger than ever. One could say it is more fluid because of people hopping from one parish to another, but the idea of a territorial involvement is certainly not dead. Father Geaney shows the kind of thinking which brings a parish to life. In this sense he merits the title prophet.

As we all seek to integrate the biblical and eschatological vision of a just world with the practical problems and challenges we face as Church on all levels, Father Geaney's discussion of the parish will keep us honest and questioning. It also will provide many thoughtful reflections and point out ways to go. No one can ask for more than that. It prods without being offensive. It raises questions without showing disrespect.

Like a true prophet, however, Father Geaney places the accent on conversion. We must become changed people, Christ-like people, if this world is to change. That comes about through prayer, through hearing God's Word and taking the sacraments seriously, through seeing Christ in others, through all of those means which are made ours through the prophetic parish. It also means rolling up our sleeves and being counted in changing our society. In his own inimitable way Father Geaney brings many years of experience to the discussion of how all this happens. We are thankful to him.

Most Reverend Rembert G. Weakland, O.S.B.
Archbishop of Milwaukee

The Prophetic Parish

Who Wants a Prophetic Parish?

This book promotes what may appear to be a ridiculous proposal: that the parish is an ideal place to start a peace and justice movement, not only to renew the local church community, the neighborhood, and the city, but to renew the total American and universal church establishment—not to mention local, state, and federal governments and the entire world that is held together by TV satellites.

This may sound as impractical and romantic as the call of St. Francis to rebuild the church. It is appealing, of course, to the incurable optimists and Christians with myopic hope who respond to a Don Quixote. Cervantes, Francis, and Jesus knew there were people out there who love to dream the impossible dream. But many people feel that from many viewpoints the concept of parish is outdated, parasitic, useless. Still, no one wants to destroy it; after all, it is harmless, a part of the scenery like trees and park benches. Occasionally, when a parish church next to an expressway or in an industrial zone cannot support itself, church and community bureaucrats order the building razed because of insurance costs or structural weakness. Then comes the hue and cry from urbanites and suburbanites formerly associated with the parish about an outrageous attack on a sacred symbol.

Granted, then, many people are deeply attached to the old parish, even if it has slipped considerably. But is it realistic to expect new life to spring from it? Well, before we dismiss out of hand the parish as a possible focus for a peace and justice movement that has possibilities with worldwide ramifications, consider some of its assets. It has meeting rooms that could accommodate people in the neighborhood; it has a mailing list, an addressograph, a listed phone number, and a duplicator, perhaps even a modern copy machine. It has women, men, and young adult groupings. It has a pulpit where human words are translated by the speaker and hearer into the word of God. Why not use for the cause of peace and justice this under-used assortment of human networks and technical resources that do not need computer-operator skills? The alternative would be to create a new peace and justice church that might attract five or ten people in a community of 10,000. But why reinvent the wheel?

By the way, while this book focuses on Catholic parishes, it should be helpful to people of many other religious groups as well. Protestant and Jewish congregations face the same issue of disturbing people's prayer time with worldly issues such as peace, world hunger, racism, and human rights. While Catholic, Protestant, and Jewish theologies and authority structures may differ, congregations are remarkably similar in resenting priests, ministers, and rabbis who try to lay their social action agendas on them. When the drains smell badly, lower-income congregations prefer a day of prayer about it, while upper-income groups prefer a theological seminar that gives a historical perspective on the problem. Congregations put clothespins on their noses rather than address themselves to the stench.

This was obvious to me when I met with ministers and rabbis to ease racial tensions during the 1983 Chicago mayoralty campaign. When Harold Washington, a black, and Bernard Epton, a Jew, were competing for Chicago's white vote, the common denominator was fear, not religious affiliation. The young man wearing a green T-shirt with his theological statement emblazoned on it, "Vote Right, Vote White," showed the church's impotency in the face of ethnic and racial demons.

In this book I am not advocating that social activists take over the church property as the student revolutionaries did on campuses in the 1960s. The appeal must be to justice, reason, and goodwill. But who does own the parish? Legally, the owners of the Catholic parish are not the parishioners but a diocesan corporation of which the bishop is the president. Since a corporation is a legal fiction, though, we want to know who the human owners are. The people who have been supporting it financially for a number of decades surely have claims. At St. Victor Parish, where I am associate pastor, the Sunday envelope users who have been paying their dues for decades are the real owners. Henry Wallenberg, who served the first Mass at the Memorial Park Field House almost sixty years ago, bubbles with delight as he recalls that day. At present he is a minister of Communion at Sunday liturgy and, with his wife Lillian, frequently visits the shut-ins. He is also a member of the parish school board. Frank Kraft and others in his age bracket have served as ushers for forty or fifty years. Ron Spellman, the eighth-grade football coach and vociferous member of the athletic board, has had brothers, sisters, children, and grandchildren at St. Victor's for all but one year of the school's existence. Young people in the parish see St. Victor's as the church of their parents and grandparents, uncles and aunts. It has been made holy for them through its baptisms, weddings, First Communions, and funerals.

Priests are certainly not the owners. They come and go: The rectory door is like a turnstile. The pastor is appointed for a six-year term, with an option for one renewal. The associates move every six years with the alacrity of a football team when the possession of the ball changes hands. Priests are seldom buried from the parish; they simply fade away.

So I have no illusions about my permanence or ownership. The lesson was taught to me in another parish in the sixties by irate parishioners who saw me as a threat to the stability of the neighborhood when I advocated open housing. My sacred calling and the authority vested in me by the laying on of hands by a successor of the apostles carried no weight in the face of people with twenty-year mortgages and the simple comforts that come from neighborhood identity and belonging. They saw me as a carpetbagger, a reformer sent in to stir up the people and destroy their neighborhood. I may indeed be loved at St. Victor's, but basically I am venerated like a visiting missionary—respected, but never a member of the parish. If I respect people's history, told and retold at the local funeral parlors and church meetings, I will be listened to, even given authority, and accepted as a leader. But I will never have the feeling of being a property owner.

One thing that parishioners do not want is someone continually calling them to the works of peace and justice. The survey of a number of parishes by the Parish Evaluation Project brought the following data:

> We asked the people for reactions to statements such as: "Sermons should stick to spiritual matters and not deal with current social issues"; or "The Institutional Church should take public stands on social issues." Only 38% felt that sermons should include social topics. Thirty percent felt the Church should take social stands.
>
> In fact, just over half (52%) agreed that the parish should even encourage parishioners to participate in community social action groups, groups that are independent of the parish. The parish staffs feel differently. Most of them (87%) feel the parish should encourage social involvement; 80% feel the Church should take social stands; and only a few (9%) don't think social topics are fitting for sermons or homilies.[1]

What do parishioners want from their pastor? People are not asking for prophetic priests. A priest on a personnel board described the results of the consultation procedure to learn what parishioners were looking for in a pastor. "We might have expected the parishioners to include prayerfulness, organizational ability and preaching ability and the like, but the two qualities given the highest priority were warmth and a sense of humor."

I can resonate with that. I feel that I give challenging homilies and address myself to the welfare poor, the working poor, refugees, and to such topics as nuclear weapons and the like. People do not yawn, but Sally Kuczynski said, "Dennis, I don't mean this as a reflection on your homilies, but the thing we love about you is your going through the church before every Mass smiling, shaking hands, and talking to the children." This, after agonizing over what to say and how to say it in a homily. This, after going to liturgy workshops and learning to improve my presidential style. I hear this as a cry for belonging, a hunger for a human community that is rooted in the Lord.

Parishioners are asking that the parish respond to their needs for intimacy, not in the sense of a close-knit family, but as a community in which they are known and appreciated for their uniqueness, a place where they can find relief from the anonymity of the other parts of their lives, and, they hope, a place where someone will listen to their story. The parish must respond to the need for intimacy and belonging before people can talk about prophecy. Parishioners need an island in life where they can care and be cared for as well as ritually express their joys and sorrows in the rich Catholic liturgical tradition.

But to understand what a prophetic parish is, we need to face the stark question, Did Jesus come to comfort us, or to challenge us? Your answer will determine whether or not this book is for you. If you see Jesus as one who caresses us, strokes us, and binds our wounds, as one who simply wants us to feel good about ourselves and live life in the cocoon we have spun for ourselves, protected from the world we live in, then you do not want to live in a prophetic parish.

But if you see Jesus as one who calls us to move forward each day and leave behind our comfortable surroundings as the Lord asked Abraham and many another to do, then you are on another wavelength. If you see the Christian life as a journey, you will want a parish that challenges you to walk down lonely paths into unknown areas of human suffering, chaotic social conditions, and assume the impossible, unrealizable goal of changing the world.

Jesus asked his followers to make a choice. When his challenge was too much for them and they walked away, he asked his disciples, "Will you also go away?" The prophetic parish offers comfort to those who accept challenge. It binds the wounds of those who suffer for justice' sake. The self-improvement parish whose narcissistic goals are to make everyone feel happy is not the parish that proposes happiness by reaching out to the poor, the grieving, the peacemakers, the people who lay down their lives for justice' sake. The prophetic parish is the parish that writes the beatitudes into its charter and uses them as the measure of its fidelity to the demands of Jesus.

"A prophet," according to Webster, is "one who utters divinely inspired words or one gifted with more than ordinary spiritual and moral insight." The Old Testament prophets were disturbers of the peace. They spoke about human problems in everyday and often crude language with the conviction that the Lord stood behind their every word. The prophet was "poet, preacher, patriot, statesman, social critic, moralist," speaking with a power that stemmed from a deep relationship with the Lord. Prophets were able to name the fatal illnesses from which the people were dying when those same people were unaware that they had accepted the death sentence passed upon them. In return for inviting the people to life, they were scorned and rejected as enemies within the household, but they would not relent on their judgment until the people faced the truth about themselves.

But telling the truth about life is only one facet of parish life. The parish is a place where people come to celebrate both the great and the ordinary moments of life: birth, marriage, death, as well as the smiles of acceptance and frowns of rejection we all encounter each day. It is a place of reconciliation where we come to accept our body, our family, our neighbors, our work, the whole world we live in—the areas in which we find ourselves separated from one another. It is the place where we draw strength from our religious tradition, our heritage, simply by dutifully adhering to its ancient creeds and directions. So why not simply make the sabbath a true day of rest from the complexities of human life and settle for joyous liturgical celebrations that establish a deep sense of connection with the people in the church and with the Lord?

I am convinced that we will not fully achieve the goals of caring, reconciling, affirming our tradition, and building a community of honest prayer until we come face to face with the truth about life. Not until prophecy or calling people to the truth about their lives becomes the linchpin of our coming together will we encounter the living God of history. The prophetic parish is pivoted on the belief that there is no peace without justice, that a parish cannot claim to worship the one true God unless it helps us encounter the demonic in our own lives and in the world of which we are a part. A church that does not engage in toppling over the idols to which people pay homage will be worshiping false gods.

Why am I proposing prophecy as the integrating element in parish life at this moment of history? We are living in apocalyptic times when our very existence as a race is threatened at multiple levels. If we believe that, it is time for prophecy. When all systems were working, we could supposedly afford to live in a parish that was a comfort station, that had well-planned and well-executed liturgies, that offered multiple pastoral services but never raised people's hackles about their responsibility for the sordidness in human life. Continuing to affirm this kind of parish that does not challenge people about the life of our society is band-aiding a world that is on a self-destruct course. A prophetic parish can be a center of hope in a whirlpool of despair.

The prophetic parish is not calling individuals to be prophetic as much as to become members of a prophetic community. With Israel, it was the nation as a people that was called to be the prophetic word of God. In a parish we too become prophetic as we reflect as a *community* on the word of God as it relates in all its incisiveness to the human chaos. We must permit the word of God to penetrate like a two-edged sword and call us to accountability for the world in which we live.

Who is this Dennis Geaney who is issuing this call? Biographical details are not significant unless they are seen as flashbacks that illuminate the moments of awareness when crucial decisions follow from insight. During the depression years of 1934 and 1935 I was a bookkeeper for the Boston Overseers of the Poor, now known as the Welfare Department. Welfare recipients lined up each morning before my cage to have their documents stamped—proof that they had done the work assigned and had paid their weekly rent. I stamped their cards and gave them vouchers ranging in value from four to sixteen dollars; they could cash them by lining up at the paymaster's window across the hall. I was employed, enjoyed life, and was untouched by the human tragedy that confronted me each day.

Then I left the welfare office and entered the Augustinian seminary. In spite of the rigid enclosure rules and the limited reading allowed during my confinement to a seminary building on Villanova University campus, I came across the *Catholic Worker*, edited by Dorothy Day. In her monthly front-page column "On Pilgrimage" she connected the Depression to both the beatitude "Blessed are the poor" and the judgment scene "I was hungry." She crisscrossed the country on buses, getting the gospel word out to bishops, priests, seminarians, migrant workers, and the Bowery people of every city across the land.

The scales fell from my eyes. I had never before made the connection between the Gospel read every day in chapel and the people whose documents I stamped as they stood humiliated before me. After that, life was never the same for me. My life was suddenly focused. Dorothy Day was encouraging people all across the country to open Houses of Hospitality that would have a daily soup line and bunks at night for the homeless. But she called for more than soup kitchens. She challenged us to look beyond the soup kitchens and attend to the structures of society that made the soup lines necessary. She called us to look deeper into life and see that soup kitchens and social reform are simply palliatives; they relieve our guilt but result in burnout. She said that we must pivot our whole life on a prayer life that creates and supports a bonding with one another and the Lord. She taught us to stand naked before the Lord who is both our judge and our comforter.

For the forty years of my priesthood as a high school teacher, journalist, and seminary educator I kept burning the torch I had received from Dorothy—as I moved with the times through the union movement when it was claiming its right to exist, the civil rights movement culminating in Selma, the "Stop the Bombing" in Vietnam, and the present peace movement.

In 1979 I became an associate pastor of St. Victor Parish in Calumet City, Illinois. Here are the people of middle America who can turn the world from its suicidal course, the unsophisticated people who can grasp the gospel message and live out the beatitudes. I choose to be in the midst of them and share with them my efforts to make St. Victor Parish a prophetic voice in our community. It is against this background that this book is written.

There are practical questions that we must face before we engage in the specifics of such a parish. Will the parish in taking prophetic stances become a political action force in the community? Jesus confronted that question for us in two of the temptations he faced in the wilderness. Is our goodwill enough to feed every hungry person in the parish and to change public policy toward world hunger? This was the first temptation of Jesus: to turn stones into bread. He did not say that he would not feed the hungry, but rather that we do not live by bread alone.

Will a prophetic parish try to flex its political muscle and manipulate our economic and political structures to suit our ideology? In the second temptation (Luke's Gospel) Jesus refused to use earthly power and glory. Later in his ministry Jesus condemned many practices of religious and political institutions but refused to head a political movement to redress the wrongs of his people. The prophetic parish is concerned about the social structures that have turned us into a consumer society that is individualistic. Like Jesus, however, the parish must disdain to use power in its own name; it must leave the human judgments to coalitions of people in the community who will devise strategies for change.

In that second temptation, the price of gaining control of worldly kingdoms was that Jesus would adore Satan, would engage in false worship. That same temptation to false worship is with us today, but it often takes the form of burying ourselves in religious practices to escape confronting the roots of suffering in the world about us. The prophetic parish thrusts itself into the swirling stream of human life in all its sordidness and ambiguity, but without committing itself to a political party or ideology. It is not a part of the New Right or the New Left but a community that enters the suffering of Jesus in the individual and social lives of the people so that they may witness the gospel in its many-splendored radiance and hasten the dawn of a new society, the heavenly Jerusalem. It does not hesitate to talk about the cross.

"In the depths of the abyss, salvation is in a kiss" is a Vatican II-era graffito that captured my attention as I strolled along the Potomac beneath Georgetown University. I was brought up to believe that salvation was in the church. Now we see salvation breaking in at unexpected moments and places, outside as well as inside the church. The church has become a voluntary association of believers. If I do not find salvation in my church, I may look to another church or look for it without the mediation of any church. Commitment to the parish community as an ethnic, cultural, or family tradition is no longer automatic.

The switch from a church of obligation to a voluntary one brings us closer to the Protestant congregational model. The overarching central power loses its effect and tends to be symbolic, pointing a direction rather than commanding a course of action. One of the obvious results is a continual decline in membership. This decline is not necessarily to be equated with a weakening of the church's influence in the world; we hope it means a more purified and spiritually focused church.

The parish is primarily a place of community worship (and with Dolly Sokol I have spelled out the central position of worship in parish renewal, in our *Parish Celebrations,* published by Twenty-Third Publications in 1983). But worship can never be authentic unless it helps the community to undergird its life with a commitment to justice. While a parish is indeed an agent of change, the change happens as a by-product of proclaiming the gospel. The parish does not have the tools of analysis, the sophistication for social strategies, or the machinery for implementing change. Its role is to offer insight and elicit conviction. It has a biblical perspective from which to look at peace and justice issues—a perspective that measures change in centuries and millennia. It has energy resources flowing from its rich tradition assimilated through faith, hope, and love.

The parish can model a just society by working to keep its own house in order. Its credibility as a beacon for calling attention to injustice is its forthrightness in looking at itself and modeling justice. However, a basic thrust of Christianity is to renew society. The realization that our own house will never be in order is embarrassing and limits our credibility, but it must not stop us from crying from the rooftops, calling the world to justice, and it does help keep us from being arrogant and lacking in compassion.

2

The Lost American Dream

The hand of Yahweh was laid on me, and he carried me
away by the spirit of Yahweh and set me down in the
middle of a valley, a valley full of bones. He made me
walk up and down among them. There were vast quan-
tities of these bones on the ground the whole length of
the valley; and they were quite dried up. . . . The Lord
Yahweh says this to these bones: I am now going to make
the breath enter you, and you will live. I shall put sinews
on you, I shall make flesh grow on you, I shall cover
you with skin and give you breath, and you will live; and
you will learn that I am Yahweh.

—Ezekiel 37:1-2, 5-6

The dry bones of Ezekiel are an image of the America that
has seen itself live the American dream from its Pilgrim beginnings through an ever-expanding frontier for its exploding
population, through its wars and Depression, always reviving
itself and coming to higher levels of prosperity with record
indices of the Gross National Product.

Somewhere in the seventies the edges of this green and
fertile vision were browning, and the GNP was not delivering
with the same predictability as the Notre Dame football teams
in their golden years. Something happened to our confidence
in ourselves, in our young people questioning our involvement
in the Vietnam war, in our cynicism about government as we
listened to the Watergate testimony of three-piece-suit executive types who saw nothing wrong in their complicity with a
president who resigned in infamy. Through it all our GNP was
holding in spite of slowly rising inflation. During the gas short-
age of 1973 as we waited in the filling-station line, we began

to see how Arab countries could push us around, then and in the future. But we did not feel depressed until Jimmy Carter was in the White House trying to please everyone and in the process alienating the rich, the poor, the employed, and the unemployed, while inflation went from crawling to leaping, from single to double digit, and the GNP developed an enduring limp.

Three Mile Island severely damaged our utopian view of science, technology, and the laser beam—forces that were leading us into the Promised Land of a push-button life of leisure for an ever-shortened work week for wages that escalate with the regularity of our Seiko watch.

In spite of growing evidence that our country was experiencing a permanent state of declining expectations, we refused to believe there was anything wrong with the system that changing the guard at the White House could not right. On January 3, 1980, we had the changing of the guard. Our hostages returned, and Jimmy Carter went back to Plains, Georgia. Our confidence was holding. Ronald Reagan confirmed our faith in the dream with his smile and his shrug of the shoulder when he goofed. The liberals kicked and screamed at his cutting back on social services, his spending habits in buying a new line of nuclear weapons whose price tag was in the trillions, while he pressed them to pass the nation's largest tax cut followed by the largest tax increase. He had the votes because America still believed that the GNP would overcome. The car-assembly plants idled as we grudgingly paid tribute to the Japanese for their work ethic, flawless technology, and shrewdness in marketing.

An increasing number of people could relate what was happening in the past decade to Ezekiel's plain filled with bones, but there was no hue and cry that we should examine the system itself. If we just give it a kick or bang it with our fist as we do with vending machines that do not work, it will deliver. The cigarettes or the coke will tumble out, or the money will be returned. If we have failed poor blacks and whites and if unemployment rises steadily and our GNP staggers, we can still get through with a little belt-tightening. The argument is built on the questionable premise that history repeats itself, that economic and political life are cyclical.

Maybe it is too soon to expect Americans as a people to question the American dream of an ever-expanding party for everyone. Maybe it is too soon to expect people to believe that the global village, which means dependence on other nations, will become a way of life. Maybe it is too soon to expect the American people to repent their sinful use of nuclear weapons in Japan in 1945. It seems that if we are to wake up, more people must be unemployed, the GNP must drop at a consistent pace, there must be more Three Mile Islands, and the Middle East oil sheikhs must scare us with future oil shortages.

Prior to the 1960s the white middle-class Catholic had a church and identified with the American dream. This class buttressed our economic and political institutions. It supported with a passionate patriotism every facet of American life except the public school. The American Catholic church provided an entrance into the church of one's ancestors and into the American life. It was an ally of the country through its parishes and network of social institutions. It provided a stable family life, neighborhood cohesion, and discipline at home and school that prepared people to turn the wheels of American industry and provide goods and services for the world. In return, people received a share of the income that provided payments on homes, education for their children, and an ever-increasing supply of consumer goods. The land of promise became the Promised Land.

Then something happened on the way to Vatican II. The church seemed an oppressor, not a carrier of personal freedoms.

The Catholic parish, which had been on automatic pilot, had held immigrants together through neighborhood cohesiveness and church organizations. But the Holy Name Society, the Altar and Rosary Societies, and the Knights of Columbus became less attractive in an era of high mobility and electronic media. The church was no longer a socializing institution for a people growing in affluence, except for the profound ritual events of baptisms, First Communions, weddings, burials, and midnight Mass at Christmas. People had little need of the parish church for daily living. Its constituency was neither the immigrant nor the oppressed. The Gospel was something read on Sunday as one would read aloud in the classroom. It was not understood to be a proclamation that the kingdom of God was at hand, not a call to freedom. We were angry at all American institutions, including the church, because they had failed us. We had never bargained for inflation, high interest rates, and unemployment that triggered a downward spiral in our aspirations for a better life. Prophetic voices could not be heard. It was not the Spirit moment for prophecy in our church or in the land. We needed to wander longer in the desert.

These were and are the worst of times and the best of times. The post-World War II era that gave us the good life began to fade. The vacuum created a hunger for meaning, a thirst for mystery, a plea for a new synthesis of religion and culture, for a church life that would relate to our frustrations as we cut back our margins of comfort. Lower voter turnouts became a clue that our democratic processes were considered less responsive to our plight.

Unfortunately, though, band-aids will not work. The liberal tunes evoke only knee-jerk responses. Only radical approaches that may traumatize the patient and lose clients can work. This book is not a call to the streets, although a worsening of our times may lead to it. It is not a call to the barricades but a call to pivot our lives on the Jesus in whose name we are baptized and who is calling us to share with one another our reflections on his work as together we try to find "the Way" through the morasses of a culture that has come to an end and to become a part of the new world being formed from the womb of people who seek him in simplicity and honesty.

We have come to a period in history when the structures of society cannot cope with the threat of nuclear holocaust. We see crime in the ghettoes and the suburbs, family disorganization, and an economic and political system in which people no longer have confidence to look to Jesus as an integrating symbol offering a new understanding of salvation. This chaos in our society motivates us to look at the society in which Jesus lived to find parallels to direct our response. When our society was unthreatened and we accepted the status quo, we simply saw the life of Jesus as a source for reinforcing the social institutions that have given us what our immigrant ancestors had prayed for. It was a way of life that offered us work for our creative powers, a healthy climate for family development, and freedom to worship. Jesus was not allowed to challenge the society that allowed everyone to climb the ladder to the bigger and better life.

In our liberal tradition, Catholics and other church people have been quick to move toward strategies for change without reflecting on Jesus and on our religious traditions. We were satisfied with the quick fix. Since 1932 the American white, middle-class Catholics of this century have identified with our liberal institutions—the union movement, the Democratic Party, and the federal government—as the economic and political forces that offered the strategies for change. But in the last decade we have been losing our confidence in these institutions. The American labor movement has been defanged, and the Democratic Party was routed from the field in the 1980 election.

In the early 1960s we began to take baby steps away from the triumphal church tainted with the symbols of worldly power toward a church that took its inspiration from the Scriptures. In the hands of radical Christian groups, the Scriptures became living documents rather than readings from the obituary page.

We learned from the civil-rights movement the power of the black churches that anchored their joy and hope as they huddled in their churches singing biblical hymns. They had withstood poverty, oppression, rejection, and humiliation as a way of life because they had learned to pray the Scriptures and find hope and comfort in the Lord Jesus.

Radical Christianity has always found its source of strength in the Scriptures, but only in the 1980s have the Scriptures moved into the mainstream of Catholic church life. Much as Alex Haley returned home in *Roots,* we are going back to Palestine to steep ourselves in its culture, to get deeper insights into the life and message of Jesus, to deepen our prayer life, to critique our individual and societal lives, and to renew our commitment to discipleship in the Lord.

Instead of cutting the Bible as we would a deck of cards to find a quotation that might touch our lives, we try to capture the central message of Jesus from which all his words and deeds flow as from a fountain. We all have vignettes of Jesus and an unarticulated vision of who he is, but at this juncture of history there is a greater urgency to flesh out a picture of him that has sharper lines and is focused on his culture. It means searching for the key themes in his life that clarify his mission and the challenges he places before us for our times.

Something happened to the American Catholic on the way to the bank. Jesus was standing in the bank lobby saying, "Why do you give your bank balance priority over me? Why don't you take me seriously? Sit with the Gospels, pray over them, and find out who I am. You need to get a fix on me and see my life and message as a totality. This requires time for reflection, study, and discussion with your friends about how I fit into your life."

We need to do what a biographer or TV interviewer does: get behind the externals of the person's life and find the secret that explains the person's life in its totality. Now, I realize that you cannot understand my perception of a prophetic parish unless I tell you how I put the life of Jesus together. This is how.

The core message of Jesus was given in his inaugural after his baptism. There is a remarkable consistency in how the Gospel writers report this central message:

> He proclaimed the Good News from God. "The time has come," he said, "and the kingdom of God is close at hand. Repent, and believe the Good News." (Mark 1:14-15)

Matthew, commenting on Jesus' return from his desert solitude, reports that "from that moment Jesus began his preaching with the message, 'Repent, for the kingdom of heaven is close at hand'" (4:17).

Luke places Jesus' keynote address after his return from his prayerful struggle in the wilderness, in a synagogue reading of Isaiah: "Jesus, with the power of the Spirit in him, . . . stood up to read. . . .

The spirit of the Lord has been given to me,
for he has anointed me.
He has sent me to bring the good news to the poor,
to proclaim liberty to captives
and to the blind new sight,
to set the downtrodden free,
to proclaim the Lord's year of favor." (4:14,17,18)

The beatitudes, placed in the early part of the Gospels of Matthew and Luke, are an extension of Jesus' inaugural discourse. Although they present us with lofty ideals, they prevent us from imaging the kingdom of God as a heavenly Camelot. The kingdom of the beatitudes is grounded in poverty, sorrow, misunderstandings and loneliness from fighting for justice issues, and disarming simplicity or transparency called purity of heart. The happiness or blessedness of the kingdom people is immersed in the human struggle.

Jesus knew his message would fall on thorny ground unless he established a community. He accepted the reality that his message was more than a crowd could handle, so he spoke to them in parables, trusting that they could unravel them at a future date; but with a small community of disciples he could speak more plainly. The electronic media are not the vehicles for preaching the Good News and expecting the listeners to understand and follow through.

Now, the parish was designed as the neighborhood community with boundaries roughly similar to those of the local political community (which in Catholic Louisiana, interestingly enough, is called a parish) that would keep alive and spread the Good News that Jesus came to set us free. Since many other agencies, including cable TV, have taken over the functions of an immigrant or rural parish, people are inclined to speak of theirs as the sleepy church in Dullsville and of Sunday Mass as a bore. The parish is a good place in which we would baptize our children and be buried from, but it has nothing to say about life. However, the thrust of this book is that the present parish can be turned around and can become a community of Jesus, or if it is too large, a network of Jesus communities. The prophetic parish has a sharply focused view of who Jesus is.

Before we begin to talk about parish-based pastoral strategies for discipleship, we need to look again at the gospel model. Jesus is baptized, struggles with his vocational identity in the desert, and announces the Good News through a brief Old Testament proclamation. He is then ready to call a church into being by putting the challenge to four fishermen to be his followers.

> As he was walking along by the Sea of Galilee he saw Simon and his brother Andrew casting a net in the lake— for they were fishermen. And Jesus said to them, "Follow me and I will make you into fishers of men." And at once they left their nets and followed him.
>
> Going on a little further, he saw James son of Zebedee and his brother John; they too were in their boat, mending their nets. He called them at once and, leaving their father Zebedee in the boat with the men he employed, they went after him. (Mark 1:16-20)

The Good News he has proclaimed in capsule form will be spelled out day after day as he works his way through Galilee, preaching, dining in people's homes, embracing little children, and performing spiritual and physical healings. However, he knows that the mass audiences will not be able to grasp his message. He says to his followers "to them I must speak in parables," because the message can be grasped and digested only by people who are with him every day and with whom he can discuss more intimately the meaning of the parables. Through discussion, correction, and the discipline of living together they can faintly begin to understand his message about kingdom and servanthood. Like a parent he shows his anger at their slowness. "Get behind me, Satan! Because the way you think is not God's way but man's" (Mark 8:33). His message needs to be translated every day into the fabric of their lives. It must be experienced in community life. It can only be grasped by a lived experience of groups small enough to discuss it and in the process bond themselves in a relationship that commits them individually and as a group to the Good News and ultimately to him. The call to discipleship is a call to personal commitment to Jesus and his message, and also a call to community or church. We call this whole process conversion.

The Acts of the Apostles describes how the church developed. It was small groups of people gathered to tell the stories of Jesus over and over in the homes of people who had a room large enough for a meeting that concluded with the breaking of the bread. The integrity of the message was held together by accredited teachers such as Paul and Barnabas who helped them relate to other communities in other cities by retelling their struggles with the faith and by taking up collections for needy communities. Traveling by boat or horse or on foot, they were able to pull together a wider church along the Mediterranean shores.

The crucial and relevant question for us is whether an urban or suburban parish with a membership in the hundreds or thousands can be a setting for conversion experiences similar to those of the disciples of Jesus and their followers in the first and second centuries. In the late 1960s small groups of people in our large cities, filled with the Pentecostal fervor flowing from the Vatican Council and experiencing a conversion, formed underground churches. They judged it impossible to reshape their own parish after the model of Acts and therefore struck out on their own. The model became an activist and elitist type church, a sect of the saved, which is not Catholic because it separates people into saints and sinners—the prerogative of the Lord alone. The experiments ended for the most part with bitterness toward the larger church and an unwillingness to make another try at bringing the lumbering old Roman dinosaur to life in the modern world as the church elders of Vatican II had called them to do. Thousands of educated and dedicated Catholic laity were lost completely to the church in the cultural and church turmoil of that time.

These people are the heavy casualty list of the first wave of enlightened Christians who were wiped out as they came ashore carrying the freedom flag of Vatican II. The bishops were ready intellectually, as distinguished from emotionally, to face the implications of what they had signed in their state of euphoria and had wrapped in what became biblical slogans.

But priests and parishioners were less than euphoric, and when their bishops returned home, they too were sobered at the sight of Pandora's box opening before them and threatening their childhood religion. As a result, everyone successfully turned back the enthusiastic but naive fresh call to freedom for our church and for the human person in the world. It would take another decade or two before a similar thrust could be made.

With this sobering experience behind us, we know that transformation of the church and the conversion of large numbers of Catholics will take place for most people only in the context of the parish that is willing to challenge and be challenged. This does not deny that there will always be a few Christians who can survive and grow in our modern catacombs as part of a counter-culture and counter-parish structure. But if the parish cannot become the major agency for conversion, we must wait until another century when the parish is completely dead and we can start all over again, using the model of Father Junipero Serra in establishing the California missions. The challenge for us is either to make the move now or to leave it to our unborn great-grandchildren.

3

Jesus' Call to a Radical Christianity

By bringing to the celebration of the Eucharist our own gift of self after the example of Jesus, we are able to absorb most fully the meaning and grace-expression of Jesus' own gift of self. Our Christian action on behalf of social justice and peace issues will then have substance and will be in harmony with the intentions of Christ in sharing the Eucharist with us. I contend that all social justice action and work for the cause of peace must flow from this radical understanding of Jesus' self-giving and our total identification with him in that saving action. . . . The world desperately needs the saving actions and grace of Christ, and it most urgently needs the authentic involvement of his disciples in the real human misery all about us. But that saving action can only have its maximum benefit and effect when it flows from an authentic understanding of the Eucharist.

—Bishop Roger Mahony[1]

At homily time at a Sunday liturgy I asked the congregation to enter a fantasy world with me as a way of reflecting on the beatitudes I had just proclaimed. In this fantasy I am in disguise at the familiar River Oaks Shopping Center parking lot. As people leave their cars and walk toward me or return to the lot after shopping, I shout to them, "How happy are the poor in Spirit; theirs is the kingdom of heaven." To a sophisticated-looking lady in middle life approaching the mall I say very gently, "Happy the gentle; they shall have the earth for their heritage." She is startled to the point of shock. In spite of the looks of amazement and anger and the giggles of younger people, some of whom I recognize as parishioners, I approach a cluster of people and say softly, "Happy those who mourn; they shall be comforted." I move on to the sidewalk. Using it as a platform I shout to all, "Happy those who hunger and thirst for what is right; they shall be satisfied." People loaded down with bundles or pushing shopping carts turn and look at me in bewilderment. Who ever heard such nonsense! I keep my cool and lower my voice and say to a young man, "Happy the merciful; they shall have mercy shown them." He is not intimidated. He merely shakes his head. He feels sorry for me. To a cluster of youngsters enjoying every moment of this outdoor theatre I say, with a smile that captures my inner joy, "Happy the pure of heart; they shall see God."

I can see men huddling in serious conversation a hundred feet away. Most likely they are the plaza security force arriving at a consensus on how best to get this nut off the property without a scene. I know my pulpit will be taken from me quickly. I turn to shoppers around me: "Happy the peacemakers; they shall be called sons of God." In the distance I see the yellow Calumet City paramedics' truck drive onto the parking lot from River Oaks Road. The security men are moving toward me. I proclaim in a stentorian voice to the whole shopper's world, "Happy those who are persecuted in the cause of right; theirs is the kingdom of heaven."

The police use sweet talk to calm me. A scene would create a bad image for the mall owners, but as a precaution they slip on handcuffs and direct me to the paramedic unit as it backs into place. The paramedics are the Calumet City firemen. I am their chaplain; but my white wig, white mustache, and beard keep them from recognizing the priest who occasionally stops at the station in the late evening and enjoys the all-male clubhouse banter as I chide them for their macho image of themselves, which is my way of preaching the beatitudes to them as we drink coffee or watch TV.

I am stretched out and strapped down. The truck races to St. Margaret's Hospital. I have always congratulated them for their professionalism as fire fighters and paramedics. "Happy are the poor in spirit." They laugh and say to each other, "What a wacko! Who wants to be poor? No pay raise this year makes me happy?" (Laughter.)

In the emergency room I give them my blessing from my stretcher as popes did for centuries while being carried on their portable throne, the *sedia gestatoria:* "Happy are they who mourn." They shake their heads and thank the Lord for my captivity. The Catholic psychiatric nurse and doctor ask me questions between my blessings on them. "What is your phone number?" "862-3200." A nurse calls. "St. Victor?" (A pause.) "Sorry, there must be a mistake. We have a grey-haired elderly gentleman here who gave us this phone number." (A long pause.) In a stage whisper to the doctor: "They said he's a priest in the early stages of senility. He's harmless. One of the priests will come over to take him home."

This is the kind of homily everyone loves. There are gales of laughter. No one believes that I take the beatitudes seriously, that Jesus is serious, or that the homily is meant for everyone in the congregation. It is simply good theatre and a relief from the dull sermons I give when I am depressed, out of sorts, or hyper with prophetic rage.

I did a similar homily on the Vigil of All Saints. It was clear to me as I was vesting that people resented being forced to go to a holy day Mass after a day of work. I thought I would humor them with my commentary on the beatitudes, the gospel reading for the feast. With tongue in cheek I asked with heavy satire, "How happy you must be when you are poor!" I was on target. I was feeding their cynicism. Poverty is a curse no one wants. I repeated each beatitude, and after a dramatic pause I made a cynical comment. Like an effective black preacher, I got the echo I was looking for. I knew how they felt about being persecuted for justice' sake; it was not something that would make them sing and dance. I ended the short homily abruptly. "There have been a few people who lived the life of the beatitudes. We call them saints and celebrate their feast tonight. The saints are the crazies among us."

It is difficult for a Catholic brought up in a Catholic culture to grasp the revolutionary nature of Christianity. The beatitudes, the kingdom of God, the reign of God have the ring of pulpit oratory that has little to do with raising children, paying bills in a depressed economy, or simply facing the loneliness of urban life. We were brought up to understand religion as a catalogue of obligations or duties rather than as blessings upon the earthly conditions of life: poverty, sorrow, and persecution. It was never clear to me as a young adult that poverty, sorrow, and persecution were paths to happiness and blessings. It never occurred to me that joy and comfort would be found in the reverses of life and would indeed become a way of life that early Christians called The Way.

I have confessed that I was not introduced into this radical understanding of Jesus and Christianity until I was twenty-three and already a professed religious. Dorothy Day's monthly column about her journey by bus across the country, describing people in poverty situations and giving insights into why we were in a depression, proved to be a religious experience for me. Her genius was to make the beatitudes come to life. When she described sharecroppers, or people driven from dust bowls of Oklahoma, or mortgage-payment failures, she was able to relate life crisply to the blessings of the Lord. "Happy are those who suffer for justice." Her mysticism filtered through her journalistic style and sent a twinge down my spine. She always had a message of hope and joy. She gave Jesus flesh and blood when on her bus tours she spoke to Catholic Worker groups and young lay people who would leave all and go to Mott Street in the Bowery of New York City. There they would work in the soup kitchen and serve on the bread line and live with and care for the derelicts who stayed at the Houses of Hospitality, known in my childhood as flophouses.

Jesus was no longer a holy card, an early morning meditation, a pulpit reading, or someone routinely received in Communion each morning. Jesus was in the midst of the people in the Great Depression, struggling alongside them to find comfort and joy in the midst of an American dream that was not delivering its promises. Jesus was more than the stained-glass windows, tabernacle light, hymns, and night prayers I cherished as a way of touching the Lord. No longer could monastic silence separate me from the presence of Jesus in the cries of the poor. Jesus was as close to me as the bleeding drunk lying on the street when I made my first visit to the Catholic Worker House in the bowels of the Bowery. Religious experience began to come out of street experience. Religion was no longer to be found in religion. It would take me another twenty-five years to put liturgy and life together as I did in the most widely circulated article of my writing career, in 1951, in the twenty-fifth anniversary issue of *Orate Fratres* (now called *Worship*).[2]

A new movement was born as young men and women opened shelters known as Houses of Hospitality—a movement not unlike the Franciscan lay movements of the thirteenth century. Without leaving the cloister or going into the soup kitchens to serve the people whom Paul called the offscouring of this world, the elect of Jesus, I was part of that movement.

The works of Dostoevski and Kazantzakis had always been cynical about finding Jesus in the Christian churches. How could I as a priest bring the radical Jesus to birth? Would my efforts be snuffed out by an institution that was entering its triumphal period in American history, an institution that counted success in terms of new building starts for schools, convents, and seminaries? Could Jesus come alive in the midst of organizational success? Jesus was playing to packed churches in our thriving metropolitan areas. But was it the Jesus of the gospel, or a Jesus in suburban captivity? Were Jesus and the radical spirit of the beatitudes and of the judgment scene being smothered in our fund-raising drives as Christ the King was triumphantly taking over in the name of Catholicism in our city halls and legislatures in heavily Catholic populated areas?

In 1943 I received my first assignment: to teach business subjects at St. Rita, an all-boys' high school in Chicago. Chicago was the American Catholic Action capital for the tiny movement of priests, seminarians, and young lay people who were thrilled by the raw gospel message not cluttered with religion. I began to moonlight radical Christianity by meeting with students before or after school.

In the 1940s I found that high school sophomores and juniors could become excited about radical Christianity. When a half dozen high-school sophomores read a passage from the Gospel and began to talk about it, they saw how they could change the cafeteria, school socials, and their relationships with the rejects and even with their families. Students could discuss a

Gospel passage about the risen Jesus as though he were present in our midst preparing a fish fry for his disciples after their night's work. It could be so real that its implication for the cafeteria could become stark and demand to be addressed.

I knew that Christianity did not have to be confined simply to Catholic Worker Houses of Hospitality. In the 1950s, still a high-school teacher, I extended my moonlighting to the burgeoning Christian Family Movement. I discovered that a Gospel passage read and discussed by young middle-income couples with a growing family in process could be dynamite. They would discover the Good News after eight, twelve, or sixteen years of Catholic education. For the most part it was bootleg Christianity, not a part of mainline Catholicism, which still used box-office criteria. Radical Christianity was tolerated because it made a few people happy. But success was still measured in numbers. The banking community smiled benignly at the standard Catholic parish. After all, it had the secret for raising money; the Sunday envelope was the stroke of American pastoral genius. By contrast, our ragtag Young Christian Students and C.F.M. were not a threat to an establishment firmly in possession.

Today we are critiquing our religion as well as our societal institutions by taking a new look at the Jesus of the Gospels. We are beginning to study Palestinian history in the times of Jesus as a way of grasping more fully the meaning of his words and finding in his life a way to help us look at the society that shapes our lives.

Jesus was born when Palestine was a province of the Roman Empire, a province ruled by Herod, who attempted to placate both the emperor and the Jewish people. The Roman government left a degree of autonomy to the Jews through a governing body of the seventy-two-member Great Council under the presidency of the supreme high priest. The Council's members were from the high-priestly caste and Pharisees and Sadducees, to whom Jesus refers often in less than endearing terms. They represented a Jewish aristocracy more concerned about maintaining their status and privilege than about identifying with the poor; in the absence of a middle class, the latter group included the artisans as well as the peasants.

Scripture scholar Donald Senior sums it up this way:

The political tensions that rankled Israel at this time were compounded by other problems. The burden of taxations, particularly for the peasant, was almost unbearable. The upkeep of the Temple and its worship traditionally demanded a tithe of the male Jew. Added to this were the inexorable demands of Roman taxation, which itself invited abuse. Some historians estimate that the taxation of the Galilean peasant may have reached as much as 40 percent. In addition, much of the land was in the hands of absentee owners, especially in the north. There was little opportunity for redress and no satisfaction in one's accomplishments.

The pressure of injustice was matched for many of these people by a burden of religious guilt. The Pharisees had spelled out the conditions for righteousness under the Law, and they were respected for their scrupulous fidelity. It was a world of ominous political tension, a world that seemed to be moving toward an inevitable holocaust, a world in which the birthright of God's people had been diminished by oppression and despair.[3]

One of the most radical statements of Jesus is hidden in the metaphor of a new patch on an old garment and new wine in old skins. "Nor do people put new wine into old wineskins; if they do, the skins burst, the wine runs out, and the skins are lost. No; they put new wine into fresh skins and both are preserved" (Matthew 9:17). The Law was no longer to be the norm; everything was to be judged by the Good News that Jesus incarnated and the kingdom that he was spelling out as he walked and talked with his disciples.

Unlike the prophets, Jesus was not a political reformer. He was calling for a whole new order, not to be confused with a political one. It was to be a new consciousness, a new way of looking at our individual and political lives that would bring about changes in the way we look at ourselves and at the society we fashion.

The position held by Jesus was radical; he denied the

validity of the system. . . . Jesus rejected all the Israelite institutions: temple, monarchy, and priesthood. He proposed to create a new society in which people could be free and happy. To attain this people had to voluntarily renounce the three false values: money (thirst for riches), glory (ambition for recognition), and power (desire to dominate). Instead of hoarding, sharing; instead of ambition, equality; instead of domination, solidarity and humble, voluntary service. Where there was rivalry, hatred, and violence there should be fraternity, love, and life.[4]

When we talk about a corrupt city hall, Pentagon, church, business, government, or union, we are not talking about the bureaucrats, who may indeed be dedicated, prayerful people who are meticulously following the directives of the institution. We are talking about the system. Jesus did not lash out at individual Pharisees but at the system: a code of laws and legalistic interpretations that strangled people.

When we refer to the system, we are referring to the web of practices that grind people down. The system is larger than the sum of the individuals who are a part of it. It has a life of its own that can outlive the work life of the entire establishment. The new chief officer of each institution may have plans to change the system, but the system has its own way of teaching the incumbent that the only way to get along is to go along. This message is not communicated by office memos but by osmosis.

When we hear about sex crimes committed in the elevators of a public-housing building, we are inclined to indict the aggressors rather than the system for which we as citizens are responsible. It is our elected representatives who in our name have warehoused these people and set up conditions in which only the heroic can live humanly. When we complain about high interest rates that result in high unemployment, we blame the Federal Reserve Board rather than ourselves who refuse to question the political and economic structures that keep interest rates high. We blame an anonymous scapegoat rather than face the fact that we may be parties to the system by working in defense plants that siphon off money that could be used for constructing homes. It may be that we are not unhappy with high interest rates because we have invested in IRAs.

We become accomplices at the precise moment when we say there is nothing we can do to change an abuse. At that moment we are accepting social sin as our way of life. Our hands may be clean when we work in a corrupt institution, and therefore we may not be guilty of personal sin; but as citizens who do not want to be active in counter-organizations such as associations, unions, and neighborhood action groups that meet, study, and act, we are accomplices in the sinfulness about which we complain. Social sin, like original sin, is something we inherit as members of a society, a country, a family, a church, or union. It is in the air we breathe, the way we think and talk, our comments as we watch the late news. It is an inherited way of thinking refined by our associations and life-styles.

It is only in crisis times—when unemployment is at Depression figures, when we are threatened by extinction as a race, when drug traffic and street violence reach our comfortable suburbs, when poverty becomes a way of life developing an underclass in our society—that we begin to hear the prophets challenging us to examine the premises on which our society operates. We are challenged to set our face against the conventional wisdom of government and corporate structure from which the media, educators, and even churches take their directions. The call of Jesus to repent and seek the kingdom can no longer be answered with the ethics of a private morality. Our personal response to Jesus' message must challenge our participation in the systems that are humanly destructive. Our struggle with the principalities and powers must involve us in counter-institutions of which the Polish Solidarity movement is an example.

4

The New American Prophetic Church

The Catholic church in the United States is being called to critique our society, to be the Jeremiah who calls us to our ideals that are both American and Christian.

A prophetic parish is undergirded by assumptions not shared by the majority of Catholics. It is not obvious to most Catholics that Jesus cast his lot with the poor and the outcast. "The preferential option of the poor" and "the church of the poor" are new expressions coming from the Latin American church's reflection on the gospel. These expressions reflect our new understanding of the poor themselves, whom we have looked upon as objects of the charity of the affluent. Now they are becoming our teachers and calling us to join with them in seeing oppression and poverty as curable societal diseases. Gregory Baum writes:

> Jesus was the merciful healer of the sick in Israel, and he summoned his followers to be healers after him. . . . What Jesus did not know was that sickness had scientifically analyzable causes. He did not know anything about germs and bacteria, nor did he realize that malnutrition and other conditions of poverty produce illnesses. Once Christians learned, through the development of the natural and social sciences, that illnesses have causes, they realized that Christ wanted them to study these causes, and struggle against them both through medical science and social reform.[1]

A study of the social encyclicals of the past 100 years reveals that these documents respond to a variety of social issues that confront a particular age. Each pope responds according to his own perspective of how society should be organized. John

Coleman's study reveals that while the total body of social teaching is not consistent and in fact is often contradictory, there is one unifying element: justice for the poor.[2]

The Roman Synod of 1971 captured in a single sentence the thrust of Vatican II and the new direction of the church. "Action on behalf of justice and participation in the transformation of the world fully appear to us a constitutive dimension of the preaching of the Gospel, or in other words, of the church's mission for the redemption of the human race and its liberation from every oppressive situation."[3]

But why should that sentence take on such importance? Don't we already have the consistent teaching of Jesus—his announcing the Good News to the poor, the beatitudes, the last judgment scene, his intolerance of the Pharisees and of Roman leaders grinding down the poor? One view holds that so much of the church's energy was spent in trying to preserve itself and establish new centers that it lost its clear focus on the Good News. Another view is that because the church has acquired the tools of social analysis, the poor themselves have become our teachers. In other words, the poor now have a voice in explaining this new understanding of the gospel message to the hierarchs.

The poor found their voice in the barrios and favelas of northeast Brazil, Chile, and other parts of Latin America, where in discussing the words of Jesus they found an inspiration to throw off their shackles and claim the human freedom to which they have been called. The thousands of small Christian communities *(comunidades de base)* throughout the poverty-stricken areas of Latin America found a platform to speak to their own church and to the universal church in the Medellín Conference in 1968 and in Puebla in 1978. Popes Paul VI and John Paul II listened to the cries of the poor in a new way.

Archbishop Helder Camara of Recife, Brazil, personifies the new church that is emerging from hope-filled people in otherwise hopeless economic and political conditions. In the film *Excuse Me, America,*[4] we see this tiny man, with a disarming smile and warm glowing eyes, gather people around him as he walks the dirt road of a shantytown lined with children malformed because of malnutrition. The film captures him in a similar situation as he talks to blacks on the stoops of burned-out houses of Philadelphia. We see him in a depressed neighborhood of Detroit (in view of the luxurious Renaissance Center), where the chance of a baby's surviving the first year is not any better than in Central America. The ghetto areas of our country are keys to understanding the link between Brazilian poverty and the American imperialism that siphons off the Brazilians' natural resources and drives them from their own land. Because we are a universal church, this data, gathered from Latin America and Africa, is being fed into the bloodstream of the American church. "We are the one body."

The American Catholic church entered the struggle for justice in the last century through the union movement's demands for the right to organize, for a living wage, and for conditions of decency, safety, and reasonable hours. In the thirties the church aligned itself with the New Deal philosophy of government that resulted in the enactment, almost in its entirety, of the bishops' social legislation program of 1919. The federal government accepted the principle of sharing the herculean task of subsidizing and administering programs to meet every social need in a depression economy, programs that had unfairly become the burden of the churches.

Christ the King was symbolized in the Notre Dame football team of the Knute Rockne era, and the Catholic high school students sang the Catholic Action triumphal marching song to that same King. The American Catholic church completed its triumphal march from Ellis Island to the White House with the election of a Catholic president in 1960. Catholics were in the mainstream, no longer a beleaguered minority.

After a short-lived burst of prophetic euphoria in the Council years and the Catholic participation in the Baptist-born civil rights movement of the sixties, the triumphant post-World War II church went into a funk. The immigrant church was listening to its own death rattle. A vacuum was being created which the liberals and conservatives would vie to fill for the rest of the century.

Something had happened to the children and grandchildren of poverty-stricken immigrants as they drove to the bank to make down payments on suburban homes and take out loans for summer vacations, travel, and college education for their children: They had lost their interest in the pursuit of justice. The blacks and the Mexicans, who were the new poor, became the enemy at the city gate. But the cry of the poor was muted by the fear of job competition, neighborhood change, and loss of status.

The seventies were the decade for retooling. The liberal American Catholic church alliance with the Democratic Party in bringing about social reforms was coming apart. The church was one more of the complex of establishments in which people had lost confidence. It no longer seemed to be the carrier of the gospel for educated Catholics and young people. Blue-collar members slid out the side door without a whimper. The symbols were losing their power.

The new church of the eighties is emerging. It knows that the political New Deal power model is finished. We are making our way through the rubble and recovering the rich parts of a tradition we discarded; we are finding new insights and directions for making the church live in a culture that is searching for meaning. The church has begun to search the Scriptures, to reassess our traditions rather than reestablish recent church customs; it has begun to reexamine our symbols and to listen to the cries of the poor in Latin America and in Africa and in our own cities. In short, the recovery of the prophetic element that we see in the thrust for peace and justice is one of the building blocks of the new church. Church membership may decline, but this could be a sign of a healthier and more sharply focused membership. A basic biblical symbol is shifting: The victorious and triumphant Christ the King is being replaced by Jesus the Suffering Servant.

Our awareness of the transition from an immigrant church to a prophetic church was highlighted in the opening address of Archbishop John Roach of Minneapolis-St. Paul at the opening of the annual bishops' meeting in November 1982. In his reference to the bishops' intense prayer and study of the issue of peace, he said:

This whole two-year effort reflects an attempt to develop a new theology. It also indicates a maturing in the life of the church. We've gotten away from the immigrant mentality we once labored under. Now we feel comfortable taking a public posture on public policy.[5]

As Molly Rush, a Pittsburgh housewife, was spoon-feeding her grandchild, she explained why she had invited a jail sentence by participating in an action designed to damage nuclear warheads at the General Electric plant in King of Prussia, Pennsylvania.

"I did not want my kids to grow up without hope, with despair," she said. "I don't believe those possibilities will come about simply by praying for them or believing in them or organizing for them. All of these are good but not enough. We have to live our lives for peace. We must directly confront the nuclear arms race with our bodies."[6] When she was asked what impact an ordinary person like her could have on the public conscience, she replied that her credibility came precisely from her being an ordinary mother, grandmother, and homemaker.

Tom Seymour, fifty-two, a former employee of Rockwell International of Columbus, Ohio, was at the table with his wife and seven children when he was asked why he had quit his job after twenty-three years. He quit when he found out that the system he was working on was designed for a first strike. He could no longer live with a troubled conscience. He would be happier living frugally and working for peace rather than for killing.

There are Molly Rushes and Tom Seymours in all our parishes. They are ordinary people who live saintly lives and await the call to martyrdom, if only they can see through the smoke screen of propaganda that tells us that bombs are made not to kill but to bring us a blessed peace. Among the people who sit in our pews on Sunday, they are the ones who listen to the voice of conscience and have the heroism to leave their homes and their jobs to go with Jesus up to Jerusalem to die that others might live.

They are the ones who know that the bomb must be unveiled as the American idol targeted on the destruction of the American dream. Each year our eighteen-year-old American males go to their local post offices and sign a declaration of intent to be sacrificial offerings before the god that has been created by their parents and grandparents. Every payday the god of war is handed over 45% of one's withholding taxes. Our bridges, roads, schools, and other public institutions suffer from benign neglect because of the ruthless monster that taxes the beauty out of our lives. It has become acceptable to squeeze a bit more from the poorest of the poor in the name of idol worship. Meanwhile, people who work in the booming bomb industries say they must stay on the job because of their children— children who may, because of their parents' work, never reach adulthood.

It had always been simple logic to American-born prophets such as Dorothy Day, Thomas Merton, and Dan Berrigan that the work of the true mystic, poet, and prophet is to see reality in its wholeness and not be confused by its parts. Berrigan wrote a poem to Dorothy and Tom saying that they had to die before the American bishops could come to life.

When Berrigan was asked if activists such as he and Molly Rush had had any effect on the bishops, he responded that Archbishop Hunthausen had to be affected by the Trident submarine protesters at Puget Sound and that Bishop Matthiesen very likely saw police arresting protesters at the Pantex nuclear weapons plant at Amarillo. The bishops' statement on peace did not drop out of the skies. It came out of the Catholic community, an American church that is regaining its lost innocence by drawing from the Catholic peace movement, the popes, and the Catholic church of Latin America.

The strength of a universal church comes in large measure from the input it receives from all its parts, an input that broadens the narrow perceptions of the local church. Its response as a universal church is filtered through a community that extends from Johannesburg to Joplin to Juneau, with a sorting-out process in the worldwide councils in Rome. That is why, ever since Pope John XXIII, the popes have been consistently admonishing us Americans about our lust for weaponry as a way of responding to family squabbles. Pope Paul cried out in Yankee Stadium in 1965, "No more war! War never again!"

Pope John pleaded with American branches of religious orders to send ten percent of their personnel to Latin America. In recent years many of these missionaries, lay and religious, from our home towns have been killed because they stood for justice with the poorest of the poor. Because these missionaries, with their on-the-scene knowledge of events, can reliably report what is actually happening, our nation's Department of State has never been able to convince our bishops that our government public information handouts can be trusted. The American bishops, radicalized by the brutal slaying of their colleague Archbishop Oscar Romero and by our government's lack of concern for human rights in El Salvador, transfer this lack of credibility to the Defense Department's handouts that tell them that the proposed 1.5 trillion-dollar budget is in our best interests. With this accumulation of facts and feelings, the American Catholic hierarchy stood before the TV cameras at the plush Capital Hilton in their November 1982 annual meeting as prophets in the tradition of Amos, Jeremiah, and Isaiah.

The meeting introduced a new style of discourse. It moved from a more strident, political approach to abortion to an invitation to its members to study, pray, and make their own decision on the problem of nuclear weapons and peace. "We are offering," said Bishop Gumbleton, "this [pastoral letter] as a guide to conscience, not the way it was done in the past. 'We know best. We know the answer.' We are trying to engage the whole church in the process we went through."[7]

It was the national church leadership, not the church of Calumet City, that met at the Capital Hilton. The church of Calumet City meets in beauty parlors, taverns, offices, factories, homes, and unemployment lines. This church is preoccupied with the fate of the Bears, Bulls, and Blackhawks, rumors about further layoffs or shutdowns, relationships at home, the medical diagnoses of people we love. But as a church leader in my community I am called to carry the gauntlet from the Capital Hilton to our city, to invite our people to dialogue with the civic leaders on issues that concern the fate of the human race or simply our human dignity as reflected in our respect for human rights. I must of course speak to the issues against the background of our lives, our hurts, our fears, our hopes, our love for our children and grandchildren.

To parishioners who do not want to hear of the violations of human rights in El Salvador, hunger in the sub-Sahara, or apartheid in South Africa because these people and these issues are too distant from our human experience, I tell about my childhood. In my grade-school days, China was a place where pagan babies died unbaptized unless we children brought to school our pennies, nickels, dimes, or tinfoil that helped buy babies who might otherwise go to limbo. Since "no salvation outside the church" was the operative theology of the church of my childhood, I have no regrets about being a good Catholic as the matter was then perceived. Catholic schools knew how to make abstract theology speak to first graders and their parents who shelled out the nickels and dimes.

In the past two decades, though, there has been a profound theological change. We have moved to a theology that says that the Good News is discovered in everyday life and that we are called to bring the world to its full human development. In the process we have changed from a church that was a fortress keeping people safe inside, to a lighthouse calling people in the name of Jesus Christ to the fullness of humanity.

This "new" approach is admittedly not easy and not pleasing to all. People may not like to hear about El Salvador, but how else will they be taught that human rights are not divisible? If one nation or one region is deprived of human freedoms, all of us are enslaved. Self-interest is not the measure of Christianity. For various reasons, the bomb may seem far more relevant to everyday life than El Salvador is, but the problems it raises are immensely difficult and complex. Some people are happy because the bomb gives them jobs in defense plants. Others object because they see taxes escalating to make up for the increased deficit caused by military spending. Still others object because the bomb takes food from the plates of the poor. Political issues always reveal a tangled skein, but we who are the church cannot back off merely because those issues are complex or difficult or seem irrelevant to our narrower self-interest.

How do we bring the larger issues of our times home to our people? Papal and episcopal statements do not move Catholics as does a parish bulletin article, a homily, or a social-action group that questions our posture as citizens, executives, or union members and challenges us to question the operative values of our secular life. The parish that does not question our everyday life will be separating religion from life, making liturgy a religious drama rather than a symbolic expression of the ambiguities the Christian faces every day in the market-place, a Sunday escape from the sordid six days profaned by our compromises to get ahead. Such a parish is following a theology satirized by Gerald Van: "The drains smell badly. Let's have a day of prayer about it."

The pulpit is only one forum for relating our attitude toward global social concerns to gospel living. It can offer only an approach, not a solution. If it took the bishops two years to establish their collective position in their peace pastoral, par-ishes must allow equal time for parishioners to study and dis-cuss the issues. The parish needs to provide a forum where people can use the resources available to the community to come to a prayerful and seriously studied stance on the world's most pressing issue, its survival. The parish's new agenda needs new outlets. I called a number of parishes to inquire how they were preparing for that final meeting at which the bishops would vote on their peace pastoral. I found a rich variety: town-hall-type meetings, study groups, small-group discussion after Sunday Masses. Our creativeness will abound as we become engaged in the issues.

5

The Parish Comes Alive

St. Boniface is a near northside Chicago church close to the Kennedy Expressway, which ties Chicago to the world via O'Hare Airport. St. Boniface was founded for German immigrants in 1864. When the first wave of Polish immigrants in the early part of this century settled in the near north side, the German pastor studied Polish and welcomed the new arrivals. The German parishioners resisted, and this led to a scuffle in the church in which the pastor was being physically beaten and the police had to be called in to protect him. Both sides won. The Polish were reluctantly admitted, but it never became a Polish parish.

When the second-generation Poles began to leave their Polish basilicas and move to the northwest side of Chicago, Puerto Ricans moved in. St. Boniface has learned a lesson in Catholicism from the altercation of a half century before. When the Puerto Ricans found no room in the tomb-like Polish churches, they established St. Boniface as their beachhead until the Polish churches became museum pieces with no one to fend them off. In the past decade St. Boniface has changed from 65% Puerto Rican to 65% Mexican.

What will happen to St. Boniface in the next century will not be decided in the sanctuary but in the meetings of the local community organizations as they battle with the real estate industry, which is eyeing the area for high-rise condominiums for Loop executives.

St. Boniface symbolizes the enduring power of the American parish. This chapter is not a sociological treatise; more modestly, it offers vignettes of how a parish adjusts to changing nationalities, neighborhoods, theologies, and cultures. It offers only a glimpse of how each generation shapes its understanding of life and church through this enduring reality, the parish.

One of the strengths of the American Catholic church has been its ethnic and regional diversity. Besides the parishes with fixed boundaries (called territorial parishes), which were often labeled Irish parishes, we had by contrast the Polish, Lithuanian, Italian, and Slovak parishes (referred to as national parishes). These latter were built by immigrants for immigrants, who at best spoke English with a foreign accent and who needed the security that comes from their own kind. The parish church was both a buffer against the harsh realities of living and working in a country where one could not speak the language with confidence, and an aid in the acculturation process. With the passing of the immigrant generation, the parish became a sacramental filling station. But for the immigrants, the parish was much more. It built schools, orphanages, charitable institutions, and cemeteries where people could find help and meaning for their lives before the New Deal Big Brother came on the scene.

St. Victor's, my present parish, honors the Polish custom of blessing Easter baskets with the food that will be served the next day. After one of these services, a woman showed me with deep emotion the embroidered cloth covering the basket. Her face glowed as she confided, "When I die, my children will fight over who gets this covering." She was explaining how four generations were presently being held together by the meaning the family gave to this piece of cloth. I dare say that with each successive generation the meaning will change and will likely be diminished. But it captures the rich Polish Catholic immigrant experience for the people who lived close to the United States Steel South Works in South Chicago. As the grandchildren move from the Calumet area to the suburbs, they will need to resymbolize what it means to be Polish and Catholic. The word *parish* must have a meaning other than being a port of entry for eastern European peasants.

While most Catholics define themselves as Catholics by membership in a parish, a large segment who tenaciously identify themselves as Catholics and believe in Jesus Christ as Lord nevertheless find that parish life does not meet their needs.

They define Catholicism apart from parish membership. Others, in filling out forms, whether an official federal census form or a hospital application form, will identify themselves as Catholics, but they simply mean that the Catholic church was the church of their ancestors or that if they ever join a church, it will be the Catholic church. They are Catholics by heritage or affection rather than by conviction.

The church itself formerly defined membership almost exclusively by sacraments received or denied. By baptism you were locked in by an "indelible mark." Through an invalid marriage you were relegated to the fringe by being excluded from table fellowship (although not every unlawfully married Catholic accepted this ruling). But cheating on one's spouse, one's corporation, or the government, child-beating, sexism, racism, consumerism, militarism, or any other "ism" never excluded one from full membership or from a Christian burial.

The *Wall Street Journal* discovered another category of Catholics: parish shoppers. Catholics not satisfied with home fare drive to other parishes in the area to find one that suits their needs, as they do in looking for any other commodity. The demand for membership by outsiders in St. Mary's of Colts Neck, New Jersey, was so overwhelming that a limit had to be placed on outside members and applicants' names were placed on a waiting list. While St. Mary's received the most attention in the press as a congregation of people who are happy with their shopping expedition, St. Victor's attracts a large number of parishioners from other Indiana parishes within a fifteen-mile radius. At the same time, St. Victor's loses parishioners to a neighboring Polish parish and other parishes that offer them greater assurances that the Catholic church of their childhood experience has not changed.

Vatican II let the genie out of the bottle. It stated that God's grace is available in all of life and therefore that one does not need to be a member of a church to be saved—a flat contradiction of the theology I had been taught in my pre-Vatican II seminary. Why receive the sacraments if they are not necessary for salvation? If the sacraments are to celebrate life, then both the structure of the liturgy and the parish life that expresses that structure need to be overhauled.

The radical shift happening unevenly in the church is our moving from a fortress church to one that people enter voluntarily and intentionally. At every baptism of infants I make it clear that these infants will make a deliberate choice at some juncture of life about church membership. It is not a presumption that they will choose to be Catholics.

This radical shift, from a cultural Christianity that understood the church as a support of ethnicity and the guarantor of salvation to a church that is voluntary and intentional, is a source of conflict for parish ministers and parishioners as their new understanding of church confronts old understandings. The tension centers around parishioners who seek sacraments for themselves or for their children.

When parents ask that their children be baptized, we ask questions about their understanding of Jesus, church, and sacraments and how they will communicate this understanding to the growing child. No longer do we baptize babies simply because their parents desire it or because it has been the family tradition. We insist on a commitment of the parents to transmit the faith to the children through active membership in the church, which is localized in a parish.

Parents at times understandably rebel or respond with passive aggression. They say the rules have been changed without their being involved in the consultation process. But our new stance is a statement of principle rather than the old rigidity of rules in a new church. Pastoral compassion allows the pastor to break the rules of the diocese or of the Vatican as Jesus broke the legalistic interpretations of the Pharisees. It upholds the principle behind the rule as having universal validity, but in special circumstances it judges with Solomon's "understanding heart."

When a parishioner of St. Victor's asks that a baby be baptized, the parents are told that they will be visited by a couple from our baptismal preparation team. It is a friendly meeting in which each listens to the other to arrive at a meeting of minds about mutual expectations. A decision may be referred to a staff member like myself, but I know of no refusals.

Maria was referred to me because she did not want a couple coming to her home. She was of Mexican descent and had been brought up in Texas where Spanish was the language of her home. She was heavy-set, with the body of a field worker and clad with a peasant's summer garb. When I explained our stance that the sacraments are not magic and that they are celebrated in a community context that implies membership in a parish, there was a feigned smile of agreement. She had heard this when she was here twice before. "Are you a member of the parish?" "No, but I go to a Catholic church when I go." "Why do you want the baby baptized?" "My family always has the babies baptized." "Does your oldest child go to CCD?" Her smile means, "No."

We simply live in different Catholic churches, but I was very happy to baptize the baby on her terms. Such people have a lot to teach me about the Christian virtues of simplicity of life and generosity. I did not push membership in our parish with her. She would feel out of place as a member of our middle-class church. We have Mexicans, blacks, and Orientals who have assimilated our middle-class church manners. The issue was not nationality or race, but class.

Sacramental celebrations will always be the major focus of parish life, but this book insists that everything a parish touches must reflect a commitment of the community to the totality of human issues. As we enter this new understanding of parish and church, we need to look at the process.

Under the old understanding of parish, peace and justice issues were dealt with through clean lines of authority. If the bishop was for or against some issue in the public domain, he wrote a letter to all pastors, to be read at all the Masses, instructing the flock on what they should know and do about the situation. The pastor used the same method on local issues. Father Maurice Dorney, pastor at the turn of the century in the Back-of-the-Yards area in Chicago, consulted with the pack-inghouse owners on wages and conditions of work and then told the parishioners how they should respond. The neighboring Irish-born Monsignor Byrne suggested in the Sunday announcements to whom the parishioners should throw their vote. Church discipline and party discipline worked hand in glove to build a vibrant Chicago church and the most enduring political machine in American history. The parish was perceived as a caring institution built on response to human and spiritual needs of particular people defined by ethnicity, wards, and parish boundaries. So the people accepted the creedal statements of the church and the party endorsement of its pastor with unquestioned obedience.

Saul Alinsky, the patron saint of community organizers and a nonbelieving Jew, reflected on the genius of the church in dividing up the entire territory of the country, states, and cities into diocese and parishes that are responsible to a chain of command. He saw the parish as his primary organizing agent or tool. A decade after his death his followers still see the parish as the most significant agency for rebuilding cities through cohesive neighbors. The parish, with all its limitations, is rooted in a specific place that has boundaries and a constituency.

What Catholics call a territorial parish—a parish that follows census tracts and accepts every baptized person within its boundaries—is one extreme; the Wellington Avenue United Church of Christ is the other. This church has 165 members who have been invited and attended a four-session class that studies *A Public & Private Faith,* a book by William Stringfellow based on the Bible and on radical politics. It is a convenanted church in which the new member says, "We convenant with one another to enter into the inner life of the community, caring and renewing each other, and we take upon ourselves its struggles with all the powers that bring war, oppression, injustice, loneliness and death."

The Wellington Avenue Church, an elitist and activist church, asked St. Victor's to join with it as a satellite sanctuary for El Salvadoran refugees and fugitives from immigration officials. Since it is not an Alinski-type church with a large neighborhood base, it needs Catholic churches like St. Victor's that do not demand subscription to a radical Christianity social platform as a condition of membership. The parishioners of St. Victor's did not covenant with one another to fight against El Salvadoran repression and every other injustice that comes across the late TV news. The Wellington Avenue kind of church can help our all-purpose Catholic parishes focus on larger-than-parish concerns.

While the Catholic church may define membership in legalistic sacramental terms, the parish buildings are community buildings. I was standing outside a certain church with a friend who was a stranger to the neighborhood. I pointed to a complex of parish buildings that covered an entire city block. The massive school, convent, rectory, and parking lot were testimony to the faith of the people who had built them during the first half of this century.

"This church," I said to my friend, "is an architectural monstrosity. The buildings are only minimally used. What a waste!"

"Cook County Hospital," my friend responded, "is an antiquated building that serves more than half the blacks in Chicago. To the people of the West Side it is one of their precious monuments, not because of its architecture but because of its history of service. This city block of buildings in this densely populated white area would also become alive and reverenced by the people if it was used in the service of the people of the area."

But today it is considered a dead parish, a relic of the past, and the pastor a museum curator dedicated to preserving the past. The sacraments have become lifeless or magic for a diminishing constituency.

Two generations ago, this parish was alive. It responded to the faith of the people. The buildings were integral to the people's lives, were responses to their perceived needs. Today the grandchildren of the parishioners who still live in the parish have a different set of needs to which the buildings might be adapted. In the past such parishes responded to needs that government agencies took over in the late thirties. But today there are services that cannot be provided by governmental programs. The parish is dead because the priests in the rectory died but are not buried. Nevertheless, liturgies can be adapted to celebrate the pain and joy of life in the neighborhood, liturgies that direct the flow of life through the parish.

The prophetic dimension of parish life hinges on the credibility of the parish as it responds to the daily pains of illness, death, troubled marriages, unemployment, which we lump under the heading pastoral care. If the parish is not caring for its members at this elemental level of life, the prophetic message will not be heard, nor does it deserve to be heard.

I was present when Father Bill Smith spoke at a parish meeting of people who were angered by his advocating rights for blacks in an area threatened by racial change. He opened the meeting by facing the people with his jaw set and his piercing eyes blazing. He asked, "Is there anyone in this room whose home I have not been to when there was a sick person to visit or bring Communion to?" He knew and they knew the answer. A silence hung in the room. He was a pastor who trudged the streets of the parish day after day, ministering to the sick, the elderly, the bereaved. These were his credentials to take a prophetic stand. He dared to challenge them about their racist attitudes because he loved them, not in pulpit rhetoric but in daily deeds. They could look at their sinfulness through the mirror of his love for them.

The pastoral and the prophetic must be wedded in the minister and in the fabric of parish life. Henri Nouwen, commenting on the parish as a safe place to face our pains says,

> As a pastor I have to say "this is a safe place to face our problems." A place to come together to confess our sins, to confess our responsibility for the problems of this world, and also where God calls us to move forward to new places. A Christian community is a community of people who come together and dare to explore their own misery, not in a narcissistic way but in order to discover the call of God out of that misery right in the center of it.[1]

Prophecy is synonymous with conflict. The prophet cannot wish it away. A friend recounts an experience he had at a 12:30 Sunday liturgy at a neighboring parish.

> I'm sure he was a visiting priest. Joe Scarzone is a wild-eyed radical. All his sermons stop just short of saying do something about the president—like kick him out of office. Several weeks ago, as part of the prayer preceding the kiss of peace, he was going on about personal responsibility in relationship to collective guilt over the

poor he sees picking for food in the ghetto area in which he lives, and about a nuclear freeze meeting to be held that afternoon in the area, when Bill, in the front row, piped up, "Preach the gospel." To which Joe responded without a bit of hesitation, "I *am* preaching the gospel, Bill, and will do so until the day I die." He finished the prayer and continued the liturgy.

Well, as you can imagine, there was some back-of-the-church talk after the Mass. I was delighted to see both of them so exercised—Joe because he believed that it's part of a priest's job to preach passionately, and Bill, because we believe that Holy Mother Church will not grind to a halt if a lay person occasionally vents his frustration and exasperation, even if he does so from a pew during the Eucharist. When Bill admonished Joe to preach the gospel, he got through to him, and when Joe replied to Bill that he was preaching the gospel, he sent a message to Bill. They could not help learning from each other. The fact that members of the congregation have become agitated by the exchange indicates that everybody has learned, that the difference in views between Bill and Joe is placed clearly in dramatic perspective. In my view, critics, even hostile ones, are always to be welcomed by those who wish to move forward.

How can a parish endure these theological and cultural glacial shifts that bring Joe and Bill into dialogue? It is the genius of the Catholic church that it survives its own stupidity as it moves through the centuries of cultural change. The parish survives everything but the bulldozer. Young people feel free to leave it, and older people have been through enough personal crises in their own life not to get overly excited about the next move. While there is slippage in membership, Gallup polls tell us that the slippage among young people has leveled off in recent years. There are no schisms on the right or left. Catholics have a high tolerance for confusion and chaos. It simply mirrors our individual and societal life.

It is this kind of parish at this moment in history that a core of parishioners dedicated to peace and justice can not only survive; they can help the old oak tree to flourish again. In Mary Gordon's *Company of Women*, a depressed group of women are on the edge of sadness as they enter old age. They are brought back to joy in their old age by the birth of a baby born out of wedlock, a baby that restores their maternal instincts. It is the Christmas story of a tiny babe radiating a love through what otherwise might be a crabby winter season. The peace-and-justice issues can be the salt that gives savor to an otherwise flat and tasteless parish and neighborhood or the light that leads parishioners out of the black night of dullness. The issues discussed in this book can raise the hackles of parishioners. These issues can drive them to ask why the parish is doing this to them. But on the anvil of debate, with prayerful reflection and action, we can hammer out what the parish is commissioned by Jesus to be about. Joe and Bill were modeling for us a form of preaching the gospel. In no way can it be done without pain and misunderstanding. The resurrection was preceded by suffering and a cruel death.

6

Social Sin: A "New" Category

A prophetic parish implies a theology that runs counter to our conventional pastoral theology. By definition a prophetic parish is not a mainstream parish. Notice how parishes describe themselves by what they publish or do not publish in their Sunday bulletins. Divine Love bulletins will include the schedule of Sunday and daily Masses, references to the liturgical seasons, a Bible study or prayer group, fun- and fund-raising events, and reports on caring ministries. St. Amos bulletins will have all those announcements but will also include notices of peace and justice meetings and reports of how local legislators voted on world hunger, abortion, and defense-spending bills. They will carry notices of the parish unemployment committee. They will call attention to American missionaries martyred in El Salvador. They will be critiquing our culture by relating Christian values to the local, national, and global scene, but always in a frame of reference that is understood by parishioners and the neighborhood.

Divine Love bulletins by their silence on these concerns bless the worst in our culture. They do not call us back to the American dream of "the land of the free" or to the Statue of Liberty's "give me your tired, your poor." The prophetic parish, on the contrary, raises its voice to call its parishioners to the ideals of the Pilgrims, the frontier people, and the immigrants, and to the dream of Martin Luther King, Jr., imaged in the Exodus call to freedom and in the heavenly banquet table.

The subject of this chapter is how to move the parish from apathy to action; from private charity to a love that is rooted in justice; from person-to-person services to social action; from flying-by-the-seat-of-one's-pants to pastoral planning; from concern about individual sin to concern about social sin.

President Reagan was elected in 1980 by slightly more than half of the 66.9% of the eligible voters who cast a ballot. One half of the American voters said, "Why bother?" The other half voted in spite of being turned off by the slick sixty-second TV ads, canned speeches, and staged media events that offered little serious discussion of issues and almost no opportunity for geniune communication between voter and candidate.

In the 1982 election the Cook County Democratic Party in Chicago cut through all the confusion of trying to sort out scores of names of candidates for state and county offices by asking people to "Punch 10." One punch for the straight party ticket ends the confusion of sorting out strengths and weaknesses of candidates but adds to the cynicism or apathy of the electorate. Since there is such minimal participation in the voting process, the policies and programs of the new administrations will inevitably engender quick dissatisfaction and a demand for new leadership.

This helps explain the apathy when we invite people to join an organization that can offer community leverage in addressing such a supposedly impersonal concern as a crisis in the steel, auto, or housing industry. The unions, the business world, and government seem to be ineffective in getting results. Unless we opt for a police state that offers us security but eliminates human rights and political dialogue, our only alternative is to build grass-roots democracy in the form of community organizations, parish-related community enterprises, and larger networks of consumer or special-interest groups that respond to community hurts that a neighborhood group cannot heal.

A parishioner was musing about the legacy he was leaving to his children. Those children, he said to me, will pay for the toxic wastes from the consumer products that give us our comfortable living; they will curse us for the Love Canals they will inherit. They will pay the trillion and a half dollars we have appropriated for military spending. They will inherit deteriorated roads, public buildings, garbage pickup, and educational systems.

This parishioner's generation has developed high-level technology that makes life comfortable for us but leaves a trail of side effects for our children. Our children very likely will not be able to afford the quality of life we enjoy—a luxury that was partially paid for by our parents and will finally be paid for by our children.

This depressing conversation left the parent in a greater state of helplessness in the face of the gargantuan task of turning around our consumer economy with its environmental destructiveness, increased cost of living, and tax bills to be paid by future generations. Unfortunately, though, our conversation did not make him want to join a community organization or parish peace and justice concern committee that would be a grass-roots response to our local, national, and global concerns.

When we talk about clean air or chemical waste, we are talking about something for which we must assume responsibility and for which we must be accountable to our children. When God created the world, the air was clear; there was no toxic waste. We have assumed the role of cocreators as we till the soil and fashion a society. In a primitive society, this role was not clear. People living in such a society had the simple, unexamined task of providing food and shelter, eking out an existence from the soil. While the Bible is indeed concerned with distribution of the goods we produce with our labor, the society it envisions is cast in the unsophisticated categories of rich and poor, abundance and need. It mirrors a simple agrarian economy. So we cannot expect to find Jesus offering us solutions for our complex problems of production and distribution.

Science, technology, finance, and capitalism have brought into the world an ever-expanding plethora of goods and services that provide travel, leisure, shorter work periods, and the possibility of extended education. It is our responsibility to make these systems effectively serve human life and to change them when they start to destroy us or our world. If we accept responsibility for the world we live in, then justice and love take on wider meanings. If I care for my sisters and brothers, I work to bring them a quality of life befitting their dignity.

There are two approaches to a justice that is based on a universal love. One approach is not to look at the system but to alleviate the pain of the victims. For instance, World Relief Services, the Red Cross, and Mother Teresa are concerned with disasters. If they took time to analyze the system that has broken down and if they worked only for structural changes, people would meanwhile die of hunger or disease, without a human response to their tragedy.

On the other hand, if I take the second approach and spend my life as a social analyst and community organizer, I will not have time and energy to work on caring projects. We are all called to the works of peace and justice, but some will see their call in terms of services and others in terms of making structural changes that will prevent the catastrophic human situations that are not acts of God.

At a peace and justice workshop the Cleveland Sisters of St. Joseph presented a very simple teaching device to help us distinguish direct services to the needy from strategies for structural change. The analogy was "The Two Feet of the Christian." The presenter drew two large feet so that each parish or community represented in the seminar could list inside each foot the specific forms of response its members were making as individuals or as a community. The point was that if all our weight is on one foot, either direct service or social change, our parish response will limp.

The presenters offered the following examples of the difference between personal charity and social justice:

Direct Service	*Social Change*
Give housing to someone in crisis	Research why housing is segregated
Transport some elderly persons to the doctor	Organize senior citizens to seek a more responsive transportation system
Write a letter to a prisoner	Write a letter to a legislator about prison reform
Treat a minority co-worker with respect and love	Work for affimative action on your staff
Teach reading	Order only curriculum texts that portray a multi-cultural, pluralistic society

A parish is called to work at both direct service and social change at the same time. The traditional Catholic direct-care organization is the St. Vincent de Paul Society, founded by Fredrick Ozanam in Paris. This saint enlisted university students to visit the poor in their homes and attend to their needs. The society was founded in an era when the Catholic church and society in general did not see themselves as agents of change. People were taught to be satisfied with their state in life as though that position had been ordained by God. In this country the St. Vincent de Paul Society has been our major parish direct-service organization. But St. Victor Parish has carried social service beyond the traditional visiting in the homes through an extension of the local St. Vincent de Paul Society called Victor Care. It has established a pantry and clothing room, and it stores furniture in several places. Every Sunday, people bring brown bags of food and place them on a vestibule table, to be taken to the pantry. On the Sundays of Lent and on the Sundays before Thanksgiving and Christmas there are bumper crops. The vestibule table weighted down on Sundays with brown bags is parish sacred eloquence calling the haves to share with the have-nots and is a sign of the heavenly banquet that is open to all.

In immigrant days, wives sent their drunken husbands to the rectory for the priest to give them "the pledge" before they would be allowed to return home. Alcoholism and drug abuse are no longer solely the pastoral problems of ghetto neighborhoods and the scourge of the poor. In 1976 the St. Victor Outreach team was formed to offer addiction counseling services to individuals and families. A staff member trained in alcoholic counseling brought together a dozen parishioners who would acquire in-service training to make themselves available to parishioners in stress. The names and phone numbers of the team members are printed in the bulletin for home calls at any hour of the day or night. Ten-week seminars are run every spring for families who are learning to cope with an alcoholic member. Alcoholic and drug addiction is often linked with child and spouse abuse and other aspects of family disorganization. In the absence of a parish shelter for homeless people, the Victor Care and Outreach team locates shelters or homes outside the parish for abused people.

The Outreach team comes under the heading of direct services, but it makes it an easy step to link family disorganization with our social and economic systems that have broken up our neighborhood support systems and atomized the family.

Direct service leads to political action. When the Victor Care nursing-home visitors could not get the nursing-home owners to observe minimum care standards, they threatened public exposure; they got immediate compliance. When the victims of Reaganomics had to quit their jobs and go back on welfare because subsidies had been taken away, a committee was formed with people from other churches and agencies to document the cases of parishioners and present them to our Congresspersons. For example, Mrs. Helen Smith, white, divorced and with three small children, left AFDC rolls to take a job earning $711.00 a month, plus a rent subsidy and a food stamp allowance. But when government subsidies were removed, she was forced to go back on welfare.

When one works day to day with the poor, one realizes that voluntary organizations such as Victor Care cannot take care of the basic needs of the unemployed and the unemployable.

It becomes obvious that a parish needs a structure to deal with government legislation that affects community needs. That structure must call our government to assume responsibility for community needs that cannot be met by voluntary groups. As people relate to human needs, they begin to see the interlocking relations with global issues that likewise affect parishioners: for example, world hunger, plant closings, disarmament.

At some point in parish history, the parish council or staff may wish to begin a discernment process that will rethink the parish's understanding of ministry in a way that will integrate direct-care and social-justice concerns.

What is becoming clear to all pastoral workers is the limitations of pastoral care compared with the overwhelming dimensions and complexity of interlocking issues that oppress us as a people. We are offering "The Pastoral Circle"[1] as a way of understanding and responding to a critical social issue that impinges on human dignity and on our parish and community as institutions. "The Pastoral Circle" is an academician's device for describing the four stages in individual and social growth through an issue that touches the lives of all.

We offer the example of Harold Washington, the black mayor of Chicago. During his 1983 election campaign he visited a white parish on the northwest side of Chicago, to which he and his opponent had been invited for a Palm Sunday liturgy. Enraged parishioners blocked his entry to the church. His inability to enter the church and even sit in the last bench became a national media event that will likely be the most significant happening in the history of St. Pascal's Parish. The event itself was the first stage of growth, *experience*. While the issue at St. Pascal's is racism, we can easily find other issues that could lead to an event: a plant closing, a decision to dump hazardous waste in a local landfill, canceling of a bus line in our area, police brutality, or laxity in law enforcement. An event becomes "a teachable moment" after the *experience*.

Social analysis is the second stage. The people of St. Pascal Parish need to sit down in small groups and ultimately have a town-hall meeting so that the story can be retold in the language of the parishioners. It would be a forum for catharsis. But grieving over the *experience* is not enough. The leadership in the community must help people to understand the roots of racism in Chicago, how it took shape with the decision of the Chicago Real Estate Board after Chicago's race riot in 1919 to "red-line" areas for blacks. Blacks would not be allowed to purchase or live in property outside the area assigned to them.

If the issue is a plant closing, the community can be helped to see that the decision may be the result of bankers and other corporate interests far removed from the local community. The alleged dumping of illegally hazardous waste in a Calumet City landfill was made at the corporate offices of Waste Management, Inc., which state and federal environmental agencies are sworn to regulate and supervise. As a parish community we are called to respond to the particular, but we must first situate the event in the larger frame of reference. We call this social analysis.

The third of the four stages of "The Pastoral Circle" is called *theological reflection*. This is "an effort to understand more broadly and deeply the analyzed experience in the light of living faith, Scripture, church, social teaching, the resources of tradition. The Word of God brought to bear upon the situation raises new questions, suggests new insights, and opens new responses."[2] On Palm Sunday the people of St. Pascal's were carrying aloft the palms that symbolized Christ's victory over death. Their angry confrontation with a black public figure told a national TV audience that the victory has not yet been won at St. Pascal's. Parishioners need time together to reflect on the gospel values to which the parish supposedly witnesses. However, when we have environmental or economic issues affecting the community, the gospel does not offer such a clear-cut judgment as it does on racial issues.

Pastoral planning leading to action is the fourth and final stage. Strategies must be agreed upon as a response to our experience, analysis, and reflection. Our effectiveness in seeing the design and following through on a course of action will depend upon the mixture of input we have had from the community and upon the commitment of the people who were involved in the process. Education or analysis without action is a luxury we cannot afford. Likewise, action without reflection will not be transforming. Without it we will become like the people we wish to change and will become part of a new oppressive structure. Pastoral planning is not a quick fix. It demands study, prayer, and disciplined action. But each time we repeat the process with a new issue our insight will become sharper, our reflection more profound, our action more incisive.

The suffering servant, exemplified in Rosa Parks, who refused to move to the back of the Montgomery bus and thus inaugurated the civil rights movement of the sixties, is the new model of the Christian who is willing to walk to work to change the system that relegated an entire class of people to an inferior status.

"Sin of Segregation" was the title of a *Commonweal* article by George Dunne, a professor in the thirties at St. Louis University. During his tenure there, Dunne named university segregation practices as sinful. In the thirties, racial segregation in housing, church, public accommodations, work, and school was simply a pattern that emerged because some people are black and some are white. It was the established order, the way society was composed and therefore ordained by God and legitimated by the church. George told me how the Assistant General of the Jesuits came to St. Louis to admonish him for his lack of prudence. "Why do you speak against segregation when you know that Cardinal Glennon favors it?" George in his youthful testiness replied, "St. Robert Bellamine preached on the sixth commandment in German dioceses in which the bishops were living in concubinage."

George was transferred, but the word was out—segregation is a sin, and Cardinal Glennon and George's brother Jesuits were living in sin. George did not confuse the issue by reassuring them that it was not a personal sin because they did not have fully developed consciences. Prophets leave these distinctions to theologians and pastoral counselors. The prophet administers shock therapy. The sociologist can help one see that racial segregation is a human arrangement that the dominant group has made and that is in their power to change.

While living in Rockford, Illinois, in the late fifties I discovered that a black family had bought a home in a poor white area. The Rockford Real Estate Board had entered a covenant that no member would sell to a black in designated white areas. When the board discovered the violation, it demanded that the member rescind the sale. At a Sunday homily with the Secretary of the Real Estate Board in the congregation I used this as a modern illustration of the gospel passage I had read of Christ weeping over Jerusalem. Christ, I fantasized, was weeping over Rockford because the Real Estate Board would be encouraging young people to act out the Board's racist ethics by bombing homes of blacks in white areas. Any real estate board member would abhor such violence, but the Board was in fact tacitly encouraging it by its convenant. I was ultimately admonished by my religious superior for lack of prudence but was not banished from the city.

The prophetic utterance brings pain to people of goodwill. Their struggle to recognize the sinfulness of their own behavior often takes decades; meanwhile, people's lives are being destroyed as their human dignity is assaulted by the most respectable people in the community, some of whom are considered saints.

What we say of racism can be said of sexism, ageism, American imperialism, militarism, clericalism, and the other isms that are a part of us, although we may not be in touch with the social sinfulness involved in them. Even though I became aware of the heresy of racism in the thirties, I am still implicated in the system and am an unwilling beneficiary. When I moved from a black to a white middle-class area, my insurance premium was significantly reduced. As a white male cleric I have instant access to centers of power denied to blacks, women, and lay people. The police more often than not refuse to give me tickets for traffic violations when they discover I am a priest, even when I am not wearing clerical garb. For one in clerical garb, procedures in all bureaucracies seem to move more speedily than for blacks and lay people. I decided on one occasion to waive my clerical immunity at a traffic court by appearing in a business suit and tie. But I found that I still had the same immunity—not as a cleric but because of my professional dress over against the long-haired, leather-jacketed young men who were being interrogated as members of an irresponsible class. Since I do not feel called to change my racial or clerical status, I must assume the responsibility to work at changing the system from the inside.

When we ponder the extent of our social sinfulness—how the most respectable among us are often the greatest sinners—we understand the inadequacy of our privatized morality. Such a morality has kept us from heeding the call of Jesus to build a kingdom of justice, peace, and freedom for all. The saints of the church of the next century will be the people who spend their lives for justice, working out their gospel understanding of the gift of faith and the commandment of love, a love that responds to oppression of others in whatever form it is experienced. This is the love of a Dorothy Day who went to jail to protest governmental rules that violate human dignity.

The gospel story of the woman who gave her last coins, the very substance of her life, needs to be reinterpreted for people of wealth. In 1969 Mary Collins, a suburban housewife, heard on the radio of a wanton killing of two Black Panther Party members, Fred Hampton and Mark Clark, by a racist-motivated police force. She drove with other residents of Chicago's wealthy North Shore to the scene of the police crime, and she and her friends monitored the case until justice was won. This was the beginning of her call to spend her life working for prison reform and for restructuring our judicial system. The shoot-out became the religious experience that caused her to give of her substance every day as did the widow who gave her last coins.

Mary Collins did not lay a guilt trip on herself for not following literally the challenge to the rich young man to "sell all that you own and distribute your money to the poor." But she found a way of putting all her educational and spiritual resources at the service of outcasts who could not defend themselves against unfair police and judicial practices.

She reads the same Gospel passage as do the poorest in Brazil and comes to understand, as they do, that we must change the institutions of society at their roots, rather than simply band-aid people who have been wounded by an unjust system.

7

Work: A Lost Identity

It was a colorful procession making its way up the aisle of Chicago's Holy Name Cathedral, but it was not like the pageantry of the burial of a cardinal or the installation of his successor. It was a people's procession. The focus was not on the pomp and status of the presiding prelates but—as it was in the early church—on the people who made up the assembly. What caught everyone's eye as they turned to watch the procession was not a bishop's mitre but a colorful standard held high by a lay person flanked by other lay folk. Each standard, held high above the congregation, bore the emblem and the name of a Chicago union local: Pipe Fitters, Local 597; Machine Workers of America, District II; International Brotherhood of Electrical Workers, Local 1859; Office and Professional Employees, Local 28.

The Chicago Labor Day Mass in the fifties was not sponsored by Holy Name Cathedral but by the Catholic Labor Alliance of Chicago, which also produced a lively newspaper appropriately named *Work*. It was the Chicago Catholic working force's finest hour. For one brief moment in history the center of a cathedral liturgy was the working people celebrating their giftedness as artisans and laborers, as extensions of God's creation—a giftedness for which they could give praise and thanks. For this brief period a group of lay Catholics ritualized in an urban setting what Catholics had done for centuries in an agricultural society.

Why did this holy alliance of work and worship, which lasted twenty years, end their liturgical marriage and on Labor Day give back the cathedral to the ordained clergy? Why have we left the industrial worker in the unredeemed factories and offices as though church were the only place wherein the Holy of Holies abided?

The Catholic Labor Day Mass represented a renaissance era for the Catholic church and the Chicago labor movement. The forties and fifties were the zenith of a short-lived triumphalism. Both institutions were into building booms, well-padded financial portfolios, and escalating memberships. It was a happy marriage brokered by the Association of Catholic Trade Unions, the predecessor of the Catholic Labor Alliance, and prelates and priests like Bishop Bernard Sheil, who interpreted papal social teaching for Chicago unionists and defended those unionists against charges of Communist influence. No one claimed that everyone in the processions was a Mr. Clean, any more than Jesus defended the practice of the tax collectors with whom he dined. Since then, both the unions and the church have been through hard times; both have been bloodied and have taken survival postures.

The labor movement had been so successful in negotiating high wages and shorter hours that its members could afford to leave the city on the Labor Day weekend for their summer home on Lake Michigan or drive their Winnebago to a state park. When the well-heeled union member was no longer struggling, the church became guilty of benign neglect. The Labor Day homily seldom alluded to the working person's greatest commitment, the one to which he or she gave the best days of the week and the best hours of the day. Neither parish priest nor theologian tried to develop a theology of work that might give meaning to getting out of bed in the morning and facing the morning traffic and doing work that was measured only in dollars.

(In recent years, however, unions have become immobilized and demoralized. They see their high wages as the reason why their jobs are going to South Carolina and South Africa. In the auto and steel industries they are competing with Japanese workers, and in the garment industry with Koreans. Working people have become more concerned about having a job than about wages, conditions of work, or union representation.)

In the fifties, the tiny Catholic labor movement that was beginning to view work as a part of one's life in God left the scene. Meanwhile, certain burgeoning student, worker, and family movements, known as Catholic Action and rooted in the doctrine of the Mystical Body, were more concerned with the Christian's stance in secular life than with renewal of church doctrines and structures. In the early sixties the time had come for the entire church to address itself to being a church in the modern world, with all the unhinging of old securities that such a move would bring to members at all church levels. Vatican II, designed to renew the lay person's life as a Christian in the world, produced immediate fallout effect on the Catholic Action-inspired lay movement. As one writer put it,

> With the collapse of the Catholic Action strategy in the post-Vatican II Church, there is, at present, no viable European or North American model for Church-society relations, no sustained pastoral mobilization of lay energies toward world transformation, no compelling sense of the world of work as, genuinely, a religious vocation, no appropriate vision with powerful leverage to criticize the imperfections and rank injustices of the social order. The absence of these creates a situation of pastoral tragedy and represents a serious dereliction of duty on the pa.t of the Church. For their absence means the effective abdication of the Church's vocation to transform the world.[1]

The initial impact of Vatican II, combined with the swirling cultural sea change of the 1960s, was a disorganizing experience for American Catholics. There were new and explosive awarenesses as people broke out of old authoritarian models in family, education, and an authoritarian understanding of human sexuality—all of which had a disturbing effect on a church that was interpreting Vatican II as the new road to freedom under church auspices. Practices and structures became part of the rubble. The civil-rights movement and the Vietnam protest gave young idealistic Catholics a new activist agenda that brought more dramatic results than working for democracy in unions, for collaboration of workers and management, and for finding meaning in work life.

With the passing of people like Philip Murray and Walter Reuther there were fewer union leaders who could offer a vision of what society could be like and who could rally the membership to work for more than a bigger piece of the pie. The graduates of the union movement moved from a cause that appealed to the deepest instincts for justice on behalf of the entire community to an establishment that was increasingly centered on its own narrow concerns and less on the rights denied to persons outside the organization. The union movement had little time or tolerance for the migrant farm workers who asked only for what unionists and their elders had fought for.

The eighties have brought increasing alienation of working people from employers, unions, and church. As orders for goods decline, employers with a larger pool of job applicants can be less sensitive to the economic needs of workers and less concerned with safety standards. In a stagnant economy the union has less clout at the bargaining table and as a result a diminished confidence in its own leadership.

The church in the seventies was straining to keep afloat as it struggled with its internal concerns of doctrine, ministry, and discipline. It was a time for regrouping and refocusing. When the church was ready to move outward in the eighties it seemed to have a new agenda vis-à-vis work life. It chose to look at the structures of our economy and plan pastoral strategies that bring about systemic change.

As a pastor I find myself caught between the larger theological and structural changes in the church and society, and parishioners whose energies are consumed in daily indignities and injustices. Here are two instances of the latter. One parishioner said that prior to his retirement as an auto assembly-line operator, when he had an urge to go to the washroom he had to work a few cars ahead, rush to the washroom, and find his pants wet as he picked up the cars he had missed. Another parishioner, an assembly-line inspector, is aghast at the willingness of the company knowingly to send defective cars to customers. The shoddy work will be blamed on the assembly-line worker, who is then unfavorably compared to the Japanese worker. My energy for responding to these grievances as a pastor is diluted by my need to work with the unemployed and to help protect both employed and unemployed from a nuclear holocaust. To be an effective pastor I must listen to the work stories of parishioners and respond with compassion, but I must also respond with a constructive approach to the whole system that dehumanizes parishioners. No wonder parish advocacy for the working person has probably never been at a lower level.

There is a more subtle reason why we have turned from the pre-sixties work issues that captivated the attention of a segment of the church: the growing affluence of the American Catholic. Studies show that Catholics were the fastest of all immigrant groups and churches to move up the educational and economic ladder. It is a human reality that the parishioners at the top income level will have a large say about the parish agenda and a subtle influence on the content of the Sunday homily. Highly educated and well-heeled parishioners are not disposed to overturn the money tables of the system that has served them well. In short, as its members move up the educational and economic ladder, the church ceases to be the church of the traditional industrial worker. Handling this situation demands of the pastoral worker the prophetic stance of a Jeremiah and the understanding heart of a Solomon.

The parish strategy will vary widely because of the variety of ingredients in the mix. St. Monica's is a San Francisco executives' parish in the plush East Bay suburb of Moraga. Very early in the morning the luxurious BART commuter train greets the parishioners clad in their three-piece suits and carrying executive cases; it returns them to their families for a late dinner. The pastor is not satisfied just to offer Scripture and theology classes in the morning for the wives or to engage a youth minister for their children. He believes that it is the men and women who board BART early in the morning who must use their organizational skills and positions of power to change the structures of business and government. The pastor and the wives who stay home can take prophetic stands in Moraga, but it is the train riders who will actually make the changes. The prophets at home lack the expertise to bring their insights to reality.

The pastor of St. Monica's wrote in the parish bulletin:

One of the many things I had to experience in the suburbs was having a huge percentage of parishioners spending most of their time and energy at a great distance from home. While I have tried to offer a variety of daytime and evening opportunities for us to come together as parishioners and to grow in our faith, I realize that to the commuter most of these are unavailable or unattractive after spending a whole day working downtown and fighting traffic.

I hope I've hit on a partial solution by moving St. Monica's downtown. Our first effort will be a luncheon and presentation on Business Ethics and the Gospel each First Friday in downtown Oakland, and if successful, we will move to downtown San Francisco.[2]

Parishioners of St. James, Arlington Heights, commute to Chicago on the Northwestern. The trains are inferior to BART, the distance to Chicago is shorter than from Moraga to San Francisco, the homes are older and more modest, but the executives take the same concerns back and forth to work. St. James has three men's "rap groups" centered around work. My first question to them was a feminist challenge: "Why men's groups?" Men, I was told, have a right to meet for the same reason women meet. St. James women have their own forums to discuss similar concerns. Men need to talk among themselves about the impact of women moving into the male work world. There is the possibility of deeper sharing with the same sex. It offers the possibility for greater intimacy or expression of feelings, especially for businessmen who are disciplined in keeping feelings and self-revelation on the back burner. It is also helpful for men to be in groups that are not focused on relationships with spouse or family.

At each meeting a pair take responsibility for focusing the evening's issue. This is followed by sharing and prayer. The issues seem to center around four dominant themes.

Work environment: What is the quality of relationships at work? How do we look at these relationships from a gospel perspective? How do these relationships affect our total lives?

Work decision: Profits cannot be the sole motive for a corporate decision; decisions have ethical implications. What is the operative value system at our place of work, corporately and individually? How does each of us resolve his ethical conflicts?

Trade-offs: Since the groups are inter-generational, there is a variety of perspectives that relate to the stages or passages we go through that change our perceptions and responses to life. The recent M.B.A. graduate may be anxious to carve out a niche in his field, but fifteen years later he may want to focus on his marriage and family life rather than on marketplace concerns.

Spirituality of work: This is the least developed of the rap group themes, but the fact that it is a concern is hopeful.

The prophet or activist may have little tolerance for such groups, when one could generate a more exciting and righteous feeling carrying a protest banner or collecting petitions to send to Congress. But the parish will never become a prophetic parish or a true community until it attends to what parishioners consider to be for them the deepest issues of life. It is only when we attend to one another's personal concerns in our work life that we can build a community at work that will face necessary structural change in our economic life. And conversely, a prophetic parish can come into being only when there is a community base in which prophecy can be nurtured.

8

An Industrial Neighborhood Organizes

Lake Michigan's breezes are not all they are cracked up to be—not if you live on Chicago's East Side. The breeze that sweeps across the mountain of coal that fuels Chicago's power plant carries with it pollutants from the shoreline of steel-mill smokestacks. These deposits form a thin layer of dust and soot on homes of residents whose hard work has contributed to the greatness of the City of Big Shoulders. East Side is a white enclave of three or four generations of people of German, Croatian, Polish, Slovak, and, more recently, Mexican origins, not unlike Chicago's Back of the Yards. The East Side taverns are the most significant social institutions of the community. They are respectfully closed on Sunday so that people can give praise and thanks for what, until recently, were the simple joys of a hard but uncomplicated life. In the past decade that joy seems to have eroded.

For these people, the American dream was modest. It consisted of a job in the mill with a high wage scale for dirty work, and children who could do the minimum at school to qualify for an entry job at the mill. It included respect for priests and sisters whom parishioners never came to know unless they got in trouble at school; it meant a trip to the supermarket on payday, and a stop at the liquor store for a supply of beer for the weekend.

Something has happened. The East Side is not the same anymore. A thirty-one-year-old former resident told me that all her childhood friends who married childhood sweethearts are divorced. The spirit of the East Side people has been broken. They never asked for much from the American dream, and the little they had has been lost. It is not that *they* have changed but that the world around them has. They have internalized their hurt and have no rational focus for their anger.

One East Side pastor captured the effect change was having on his parishioners.

Standing at the altar one Sunday during Mass, I was conscious of being frustrated at the "distance" I felt. It wasn't so much a physical distance among people, although that "body language" was there in a half-filled church with individuals standing alone and distant from one another. It was more an emotional and spiritual distance. The image that immediately came to mind was that of 300 people standing in their own individual glass phone booths—present, visible and moving correctly through the ritual but isolated, at arm's length, enclosed within their own private lives. Superman is not the only individual with a penchant for phone booths![1]

These people are not aware that they are perverting the American dream by burning incense before false gods that eat away at the fabric of the urban neighborhoods that made our country great—neighborhoods where people laughed, fought, and made up. With no Molly Rushes or Tom Seymours to confront them with their nightmares by naming the false idols, the Eastsiders walk through the streets with glazed eyes, pick up hymnals in their churches, but cannot sing. "Where there is no vision, the people perish."

Our churches are called to preach against false gods. But that is not what the majority of parishioners want to hear. They come to church on Sunday to receive a word that will help them deal with an alcoholic spouse, adultery, a child-beater, a spindle of unpaid bills, a floating kidney. Everyone has a physical pain or heartache and needs a consoling word. There is a school of thought among homilists that says we must address the congregation's pains and aches; that is the only thing they want to hear. It is the formula for the "successful" pastor who gives people what they want rather than what they need. But what may really be needed is to address the nightmares that lie beneath their heavy drinking, their spouse- and child-beating, and their psychosomatic pains in bodies that cannot fight off infections because of unrecognized stress.

If the false god is an economic system that has life-and-death power over people's lives, it cannot be conquered by individual Christians or even by a parish. The false god demands a biblical or prophetic response from all the religious groups—Catholic, Protestant, Jewish—and from others who believe in a God who calls us to vindicate the rights of all oppressed people. The response of our Calumet region, which includes the East Side and Calumet City, was triggered by an event that has come to symbolize all our hurts.

March 28, 1980, was Black Friday in the Calumet region of Lake Michigan, which produces one third of the steel of the country and which gives the region its identity. On orders from Chase Manhattan Bank, Wisconsin Steel padlocked its plant, locked out 3,300 steel workers, put their pensions in jeopardy, and canceled their health insurance. Furthermore, the workers soon found out that their last two paychecks had bounced. One could imagine the dominoes falling in the next few years—unless the community raced to protest sudden plant closings and mills going south for lower taxes and cheaper labor.

A small group of priests and ministers came together to plan a community response to protect the future of a community that could lose its high-paying jobs that support proud ethnic enclaves—jobs that could be replaced by a service economy symbolized by the Big Mac that hires part-time people at close to the minimum wage and offers no fringe benefits. The first public meeting brought out a member of the U.S. Congressional Steel Caucus, the Catholic bishop of Gary, and the Vice-President of Inland Steel. It drew from all segments of the community except the people whose lives were on the line. Experienced community organizers were hired to put together local congregations.

I was crestfallen when the St. Victor chapter I had helped form drew fewer than forty people, including staff and those parishioners who have a compulsion to be present at every parish meeting. Not one of the 150 Republic Steel workers to whom I sent invitations showed. We could not convince the steel workers, employed or unemployed, that we could be the lever that could lift the community back to its proud position.

The impetus for the Calumet Community Religious Conference (CCRC), which we put together, came from the ecumenical coalition organized after the plant closing in Youngstown, Ohio. Their response was more ambitious than ours. It included the banks, unions, and the federal government, and was headed by a popular and enlightened Catholic bishop, James Malone. After four years of untiring work, Bishop Malone reflected:

This was one of my greatest disappointments. For whatever reason, many good, knowledgeable members of our faith community did not come forward to offer their support. This response was from a diocese that has encouraged all manner of post-Vatican II renewal movements, many of which claim to develop lay leadership.

The social gospel can be made real only to the extent that we take advantage of those situations which we face in our everyday lives. First our brother's concern for the rights of the workingman and the well-being of his family in today's economy must be translated into action in the day-to-day world. . . .

I tell you this is my way of illustrating our greatest failure. Our people have not been moved by the social justice message even though they knew about it. They have studied it to some extent and they endorse it in principle. As I went from parish to parish during this time, people let me know that they were aware of what was happening. Some even expressed satisfaction that "the church" was doing something about the mill's shutdown. But they did not get involved. They did not see themselves as "the church," at least in this practical instance. . . .

We have had specific programs in our diocese, especially after Vatican II, to increase people's awareness of social needs. Some 5,000 took part in one such program and another 8,000 in a synod process which also included discussion on Christian responsibility to meet social justice needs. If we had been able to involve about 10 percent of those who took part in the study sessions, we might have been able to make a difference in the ultimate result.[2]

The Calumet and the Youngstown responses to plant closings that had devastating effects on these communities showed that people felt overwhelmed. The churches were unable to mobilize the community. The leap from studying Vatican II documents on justice to actions that demanded huge commitments of time and energy seemed beyond their ability.

The Calumet Community Religious Conference was tilting at windmills or baying at the moon in thinking that it could bring the steel industry to turn back the clock to the good old days of full employment, joy in our homes, and good fellowship in our taverns. The Archdiocese of Newark came up with RENEW, a formula for parish renewal that it hoped would sensitize people to their responsibility for the world in which they worked, even though they did not make the world its focus. RENEW is now a national parish renewal program aimed at turning people outward.

At St. Clare Parish in Chicago, 265 people in 28 groups gathered for a meeting of RENEW. This portion of the program was centered on justice. The discussion starter was "Relate some experience of unjust treatment in your past life that helps you to begin to appreciate the poverty of the ghettos or the third world."[3] I arrived at the rectory late in the evening when priests were comparing notes after attending RENEW meetings. They were dealing with their own and the people's frustrations with this segment of the program. Even with the Good Samaritan reading as the backdrop for this discussion, the people were tongue-tied. They could not think of injustices in their lives that would help them understand the injustices of people different from themselves. The priests had the same difficulty as did the parishioners. The discussion starter left them confused and overwhelmed.

RENEW brings people together in their homes to discuss a Scripture passage as a springboard for talking about their own gospel perspective on daily life. St. Clare's was into its third six-week semester when the subject of justice was introduced. It is difficult for Catholics who have been spoon-fed a privatized morality to suddenly relate the Scriptures to the social injustices they experience. Social justice was not included in the catalogue of sins they were taught for examining their conscience in preparation for the sacrament of reconciliation. Love is a subject about which we are all eloquent. When our homilies or small-group discussions center around love, energies are released. Our tongues are loosed. We can talk about it on every level—love in bloom, love requited, love rejected, the absence of love that makes us destructive or apathetic, the presence of it that has us singing and dancing to its tunes.

But justice does not turn people on. It is the language of idealists, angry people, complainers, and trouble-makers. I am sure that for the parishioners of St. Clare's white, middle- and lower-income neighborhood it brought back the memories of Martin Luther King, Jr., marching in their area, Gage Park High School racial incidents, the black ghetto a half mile away, the Vietnam protesters, the Hippies and Yippies of yesteryear, our high taxes that provide food stamps for people on welfare who "drive to the supermarket in Cadillacs and wear fur coats." But the kind of justice implied in the discussion starter is not about getting the right change when you make a purchase. It implies an awesome gamut of human relations that jam our emotional computer system.

The church has preached a love unrelated to our life as citizens. Now it says that justice is at the heart of the gospel message and of the church's mission. Can we reasonably expect people to make the quick switch we seem to be asking?

In this era of transition from the immigrant parish to a parish in a secular society there are no perfect programs. While RENEW sees its goal as developing parish leadership that is motivated by the Scriptures, it does not attempt community, neighborhood, or economic renewal.

Can the parishes of an area begin the work of totally renewing an area like the heavily industrial Calumet region? A second generation of community organizers, heirs of the forty years' experience inspired by Saul Alinsky, are telling church people across the country that the parish is the only hope for renewing neighborhoods and cities. They point to successes in San Antonio and East Los Angeles and to beginnings in

San Francisco and San Jose. They have parted company with the conflict model that organizes by identifying and vilifying an enemy as a way of solidifying one's own groups. In the eighties they seem willing to let the church bring its biblical critique to the formation of parishioners who will be the de facto community organizers.

Community organization begins with an assessment of the neighborhood by door-to-door conversation with residents and by holding town-hall meetings or other forums where people can find their voices and overcome their apathy and defeatism. Its goal is not development of persons as individuals but the development of persons through community response to life. It is centered around secular concerns rather than sacraments, and ultimately hopes to give a richer meaning to sacraments as celebrations of life. We are not posing a choice between RENEW and community organization, but offering models that people can appraise in forming their own models that may not resemble either. Packaged programs are for the uncreative or those who cannot devote the time to researching and planning. The ideal is a creative response from people excited about finding new ways to respond to the neighborhood with one eye fixed on the gospel.

9

A Peace and Justice Commission

A prophetic parish needs an umbrella organization in which people can gather their social concerns, sort out their priorities, and build action groups around particular issues. "Peace and Justice Commission" is a common designation for such groupings.

A commission can call people to rally around issues to which they feel called and can offer them a parish forum in which they can present their case to the parish. A peace and justice commission can have the long-term effect of alerting the whole parish to issues of which parishioners have little awareness. This is done through projects, pulpit announcements, and parish meetings called by the commission to focus particular concerns. Probably the commission's greatest effect on the parish is the visibility it gives to a small group of parishioners who have a new consciousness about issues that seem far removed from the ordinary parishioner's orbit of concern. The commission can lead to education and awareness by osmosis.

Each parish peace and justice or social concern commission will have a unique history. The St. Victor Peace and Justice Commission is offered simply as a case history. The call for the commission was issued in the weekly bulletin by the pastor on June 25, 1981. It read:

> Surely there is not enough space in this column to tell all the stories of love which verify ours as an authentic Christian community. Let me sum it up in the following way: the hungry are fed, the poor clothed, the distressed counseled, the grieving comforted, the sick in hospitals and nursing homes visited, the elderly reminded of their importance, the addicted treated, the separated and divorced welcomed and renewed, the stranger taken in as

one of our own. We are far from perfect but surely we are trying to obey the command of Jesus: "Love one another as I have loved you."

It is because I recognize how well we are doing in this regard that I feel it necessary to point out that we are doing little in another area, the area of concern outside our own immediate community. True, we do send a good amount of money each month to an inner-city parish, and we did send lay missionaries to the South Pacific. But still I suspect that our Christianity is too parochial, too concerned with local needs and not enough concerned with issues and problems which are regional, national or global in scope. We must be concerned about the steel crisis, the nuclear arms race, the oppression in El Salvador, world hunger and poverty, human rights, etc. . . .

We cannot, all of us, study world issues of justice and peace; even less can all of us do something about these issues individually. But it would be a valuable ministry for some of us! We could gather to discuss and pray over these concerns. We could report back to the parish our findings and conclusions. If and when the Spirit moves us to do something concrete, we could invite our fellow parishioners to participate.

The first two meetings, which drew about twenty parishioners each, covered a spectrum ranging from those who are simply consumers of all parish services to those who were well informed and dedicated to specific justice issues. Committees were formed around the arms race, issues such as abortion, El Salvador, flooding in Calumet City, the handicapped, world hunger, the Calumet Region economic crisis, and gun control. Each committee was asked to do its homework and make a presentation to the full commission. Some committees met but lacked the resources to translate their concern into study and action. We will here confine our report to disarmament, world hunger, unemployment, and the handicapped.

Disarmament. The Arms Race Committee of the Peace and Justice Commission evoked the deepest initial interest. It began with four people of diverse ideologies, the right and left extremes. After months of argument it was agreed that the nuclear freeze was the least common denominator upon which all could agree as a starting point in peace education for the committee and the parish. A public meeting was ultimately held, and the proposal was made to acquire petitions from citizens to present to the City Council asking that it advise our state and federal legislatures to support a freeze. Since it was the work of a parish committee, it was not a commitment of the parish and therefore did not raise the hackles of parishioners who were not in favor of the freeze or were opposed to a parish engaging in a discussion that had political implications. A door-to-door campaign, presentations to church organizations, and a sidewalk petition signup one Sunday after Masses provided 2,000 signatures, which convinced the City Council that our position represented the overwhelming majority of the city. This was tested in the November 2, 1982, referendum on the freeze. Cook County voted 71% in favor of the freeze, our township 63%, and the 29 precincts within our parish 73%.

Our attitude toward the freeze is captured by George F. Kennan, former Ambassador to the Soviet Union:

> While a freeze of this nature is naturally open to criticism on the part of those who take seriously the various statistical comparisons between Soviet nuclear arsenals and our own—and while it would be only the merest beginning of what really needs to be done—the demand for it serves very well as a symbol and rallying point for the anxieties that inspire it.[1]

St. Victor Parish and the American people through the initial consciousness-raising campaigns of the nuclear freeze movement have completed phase one. The next phase is an educational program that gives us a broader understanding of our seduction by idols. Kennan continues:

> We have to recognize that we are further from our goal than we thought. The road is going to be longer and harder than it first appeared. We must lay our plans with a view to their producing their results in a matter of years, not months. And the central element in these efforts must be an educational campaign of massive dimensions. In

the case of the nuclear arms race the initial focus must be on these deficiencies in our society and in our political system that have made it so difficult for us to deal sensibly and constructively with it.[2]

The educational program must be carried on at all levels. The bishops' 1983 pastoral letter on peace and nuclear arms is a basic study guide for adult education programs in seminaries, colleges, and parishes. It contains a most astute current theological refinement and reflection on the issues of peace in a highly complicated society. While it commends pacificism as a legitimate interpretation of the gospel, it does not canonize it. It seeks to explore sensitively all the questions related to an adequate national defense.

World Hunger. The world refugee problem is just another TV documentary to most parishioners—one more insoluble problem of other people that does not touch their own lives. The Victor Care Committee tackled the world refugee problem, not with a bombardment of films, statistics, charts, and graphs, but by informing the parishioners that it was assuming responsibility for relocating in the parish a Thai or Vietnamese refugee family or Polish political exiles.

This announcement set scores of people into motion to provide complete home furnishings and a stocked pantry and refrigerator before the family arrived at the airport. The day of arrival created the excitement of a homecoming. Eventually the family was introduced to all the parishioners at the Sunday Masses.

This is an opening to help people grasp the issue of refugees. Education, critical analysis, and gospel reflection are simply exercises unrelated to life until the participants become emotionally involved in the human concern underlying the reflection. Without this entry point, education remains at the level of mass media information or of going to school to establish job credentials or status.

How can a parish make real the world hunger problems in such a way that parishioners know that the committee is more than a discussion group? How can people of Polish ancestry realize that the hunger in sub-Sahara is more acute and needs to be addressed more vigorously than hunger in Poland since the breakdown of Solidarity? Many of our parishioners have relocated in our white reservation to escape from neighbors of African ancestry.

The World Hunger Committee of the St. Victor Peace and Justice Commission that addressed these questions is ecumenical in membership. It includes, for example, a neighboring minister's wife. It is the offspring of a man who lives outside the territorial limits of our parish. Bill, whose large family is grown up and out of the household, is committed to the belief that the Lord is revealed in the poorest and most oppressed. He quotes Matthew 25: "I was hungry and you gave me food. . . ." He believes that we must begin where people are the most hungry, the parts of the world where starvation is greatest. This runs counter to the conventional Christian wisdom that "charity begins (and ends) at home." Bill is a persistent man. After his first slide presentation of Bread for the World, many admired him for his work, but no one volunteered to join his crusade. However, with persistence he nine months later promoted a method whereby everyone at the Sunday Masses could respond in a practical way, other than by money offerings, to our responsibility as a wealthy nation to poorer nations.

Bread for the World is an American Christian citizens' movement involved in the church's mission to work for social justice. It is a national political lobby of 40,000 members, deeply rooted in Scripture, who work for legislation that is beneficial to the hungry of the world. In the past decade Bread for the World has been responsible for important hunger-related legislation, including the Right to Food Resolution, the Human Rights-Human Needs Amendment, the Emergency Grain Reserve, the National Grain Reserve, U.S. Nutritional Monitoring, the Hunger and Global Security Act, and several domestic food programs.

During three Sundays of Lent, lengthy bulletin articles presented the case for responding to the 6.3 million African refugees vulnerable to starvation, malnutrition, and disease. The response was Bread for the World's "offering of Letters Campaign—Africa." After each Mass, people went to the parish hall to write letters to Congresspersons about specific bills to support a reform of our African foreign aid support. World hunger must ultimately be addressed in our legislative halls, where famine-prevention measures can be designed. Simply responding through private charities after famine has occurred is obviously inadequate. Parishes that sustain "an offering of letters" campaign year after year will ultimately raise the consciousness of the entire parish to a sense of responsibility for the whole human family. A committee of three or four people is large enough to keep this awareness above the surface.

Unemployment. Unemployment both intensifies existing family disorientation and breeds its own set of problems. When our parish unemployment figures climbed above ten percent, we sent out the call to all unemployed people to meet weekly to discuss their situation. We quickly learned that people do not want to be identified as unemployed. It is an affront to one's dignity, a source of shame to admit being unemployed. For men, work is closely related to their self-image, and they tend to hide. A second mistake was to refer to it as a group that discusses one's feelings about unemployment.

Who wants to talk about negative feelings about self? It was a learning experience for me. Executive types may respond to meetings that have therapeutic overtones, but blue-collar workers are repulsed by introspective techniques. After a shaky start we were able to make course correction. We changed the name to Job Search Committee and focused on building a parish skills inventory and listing skills needed by home owners. A few of the spin-offs were a canning seminar, home-repair seminars, and the beginning of a food co-op. The committee has also become a rap group where people remain for hours after the meeting, drinking coffee. The committee has become a microcosm of another type of economy that can sustain people during a lengthy depression and help them move into community relationships that are both emotionally supportive and based on a healthy mutual economic interdependence.

In the minds of parishioners the parish exists, like City Hall or a social service agency, to meet the immediate needs of its constituents. We are arguing that the more loving or charitable direction of the parish would be to devote its energies to raising awareness of the underlying *causes* of the immediate problems without neglecting the first-aid services that must be administered today.

Shall we try to clean up the pollution downstream, or shall we discover what's causing the pollution and prevent it from entering the stream? This approach implies a theology that is swiftly developing in the Roman Catholic church—a theology that relates love and justice.

The Handicapped. The Handicap Committee is an example of how a Peace and Justice Commission can move the entire parish. A Handicapped Awareness Group existed in our area before we formed our Commission. It was a regional branch of a network of such groups throughout the metropolitan area. It sponsors religious and social events with the complicated and carefully planned logistics of moving an army. Many of the leaders of our regional group worship at St. Victor's, and some became members of this Peace and Justice Committee. Through this linkage the entire Peace and Justice Commission used its resources to raise money by selling badges outside of church to send representatives to the Disabled Americans' Rally for Equality (DARE) in Washington, D.C.

One of the points of frustration for the handicapped was St. Victor's front entrance; it has ten steps built in cement and extending from the street to the church. The side entrances have similar problems. At first we encouraged our handicapped to go to the close-by parishes that have buildings at street level. It was like telling them there was no room for them in their own church. The cost and architectural problems seemed insurmountable, but the presence of the handicapped kept our imagination and dialogue alive.

When a parishioner became too feeble to climb the steps with help and had to sit in the car while his wife worshiped, we found a collapsible wheel chair in which four ushers could lift him to our floor level and one could wheel him down the aisle to where he could sit next to his wife. When he is carried up the steps and wheeled down the aisle each Sunday, five hundred people are having their consciousness raised to a new awareness of the needs of the handicapped.

Through a Peace and Justice Commission a parish can move from rhetoric about issues to actions that change the lives of individuals and of the community.

10

Women in a Male Church

If women are to have a voice in the church, be included in its decision-making processes, be included in all ministries, and take a turn at sitting in the presider's chair at the Eucharist, we are calling for a revolution. Men are in charge of the church. They support their claims by referring to theologies written by males reflecting male experience, to traditions stemming not from the gospel but from patriarchal cultures perpetuated by males in a so-called egalitarian society.

This chapter is not a theological refutation of the dominant male theology, nor is it a call to women to bring their rocks to the barricades. It is more modest. It is simply an attempt at expanding awareness of what we might do in our parish, the branch office of a male hierarchical church. I hope the reader will see sexism in the church as one more idol that must be confronted and toppled over, another demon that must be exorcised as we expand our view of social sin, continue the conversion process, and struggle to make all things new in Christ.

An underlying assumption of this chapter is that the male clerical priesthood of which I am a card-carrying member is the enemy. As a group we are loved by parishioners and seen as caring people, but expecting us to lead the parade for change is as unreal as expecting the Pentagon officials to lead the peace marchers down Pennsylvania Avenue from the White House to the Capitol. It is women who experience the oppression; the male experience of women's subordination is vicarious. Women must take the leadership in raising consciousness. We males need to be relentlessly pushed by women, but we also need women to be empathetic to our struggle to let go.

It is for this reason that I offer as an opener the following case study.

The River Oaks clergy of the southeastern part of the Chicago archdiocese meet the first Monday of the month, from noon to two for a lunch spiced with clerical camaraderie and followed by a business meeting. The principal agenda item of one meeting was whether to invite other full-time staff members to our meetings.

Someone raised the issue of inviting non-clerical members—in other words, women. I offered a compromise of inviting them to every other meeting. A certain fierce pair of eyes confronted me for my wimpy attempt to compromise the gospel of Jesus Christ. Their owner was joined by two pastors who took a no-compromise stance.

The argument for admitting them was that we have no credibility with our women staff members if we continue to exclude them from the pastoral decision-making process of the clergy group. Another argument was that the women needed the same support that we give to one another. A pastor and associate laid down a trump card in saying that they would not come back if there was a compromise. I suggested that, on the other hand, some would never come back if we broke up "that old gang of mine." With no negative votes it was agreed to have open meetings henceforth and forever.

It may be that the River Oaks cluster, because of their refusal to insist that women sit in the back of the cluster staff bus, will be renamed the Rosa Parks cluster. This move may be the volcanic tremor that signals an eruption of our twenty-century-old male-dominated church—an eruption that will bury forever our patriarchal approach to our decision-making process that excludes over half the church. But I doubt it.

The previous summer I had participated in a four-day peace and justice workshop at which the presenter opined that by the end of the century all educated women in this country would be lost to the church. Toward the end of the conference a middle-aged, sophisticated lay woman was asking herself if it was worthwhile for her to put her energies into a church that has no place for the contribution of creative women.

Why this attitude toward women, and where is it leading? The attitude is, of course, part of the long history of male repression of women, a repression that has been so sanctified that it is seen as ordained by God. This repression is especially exercised against those women whom priests have trained to serve them: sacristans, housekeepers, secretaries, staff members. Few priests would expect such women to lead the parade against men who are not only their employers but their anointed spiritual leaders as well. Nor would many priests expect any change in the loyalty of other women who are at the core of church activities. After all, as priests look out at the congregation, they see that women are still a majority in the pews. What priests may not realize, though, is that as women's new consciousness of their worth builds every day in our secular culture without a unified movement, without spectacular events, without a revolution, more and more women are leaving by the side door.

Listen to Dolores Curran, parent, author, and columnist:

> From my work with families, I perceive that the Catholic laywoman is no longer interested in a church that devalues her time, her intelligence, her role in church and marriage, and her personhood. Only those parishes and dioceses (and movements) that are recognizing the immense potential of "ordinary women" and giving them permission to use their giftedness to minister in viable ways are retaining the allegiance of their gifted women.
>
> At one time, the church was the only vehicle open to women who wanted to use their talents beyond the home. The world was closed to them. Now the reverse is true. The world is opening and the church all too often remains calcified in the traditional children/church/kitchen role assigned women. The older, less transient, often rural parishes tend to retain this latter model. Their women seem more content with bazaars, potlucks and CCD teaching.
>
> But in other parishes and dioceses the Women's Movement is having a visible impact. Career wives and mothers have to have a good reason to get involved in church, perhaps some form of family, social, or liturgical ministry. They aren't trying to fill their time or fulfill a need

through their church. Many are interested only if they can share the activity with their spouses and/or families. They don't want an already fragmented family calendar stretched even further.[1]

This was a thesis I accepted intellectually, but it did not become a part of my lived experience until I attended a board meeting of the Association for the Rights of Catholics in the Church. The eighteen participants were equally divided between men and women. For a day and a half I listened with new intensity to educated women talk about their sexuality and how they hear it talked about in a male church. I presume I will never experience a female pope telling me how a man experiences his manliness as women hear a male pope speak to them about their nature as though it were apart from human nature.

It was the parity of men and women around that table that radicalized me. Each of us was a fragmented, broken person, seeing reality through a dark glass, affirming our own experience but not claiming that it is more than a sliver of the whole. Women have no more corner on wisdom than do men. Wisdom comes from a community of men and women locked in a soul-searching, prayerful dialogue.

I felt we were modeling church as we sat and listened in awesome respect to one another. Never again can I sit at a priest's meeting or observer box of the bishops' meeting and feel that the truth about Jesus, the church, and human life will ever emerge in a significant way in these forums. No longer is a one-sex filter adequate for me.

A young colleague began his homily imaging the heavenly banquet table as mirroring the relationships that exist in the congregation. The heavenly banquet captures our becoming one in life's variety of relationships—relationships that are symbolized in the eucharistic assembly. It suddenly struck me that the gospel image of the wedding feast captures what our parish is called to be. Who ever thought of a wedding feast of all males or all females? The joy we experience at a wedding reception is the experience of men and women enjoying one another's presence without reference to age, sex, or status.

Grandmother is dancing with grandson. The in-laws are talking to the outlaws. A moratorium or truce has been declared on all sibling rivalry and on the macho and clinging-vine sexual games people play. The wedding feast does not deny our differences: male and female, engaged, married, divorced, deserted, gay, lesbian, celibate, single, lay, religious, priest, deacon. It is a larger perspective of life than the statuses, roles, and labels we lay on each other. Once the wedding feast is rolling, it is our humanity that makes us one.

At a wedding reception of a fireman's daughter to which I was invited as the witnessing priest and the chaplain of the city's fire department, I saw the exaggerated macho banter of the firemen melt in the presence of their wives. Since the party is a modeling of the kingdom, I asked a fireman who had withdrawn from the church if he experienced the presence of the Lord on this joyful occasion. His face lit up. But when I said, "People are probably closer to the Lord tonight than they will be tomorrow morning at Mass," he frowned disagreement. He insisted that God is in church. Although this man is not going to return to the church, he prefers to nurture his guilt for staying away rather than reject his third-grade teacher and affirm his present experience as an epiphany.

Discipleship is another gospel image that undercuts the human barriers we construct to keep us from relating to one another as equals. Jesus' primary call to us is not to marriage, virginity, or any of the statuses out of which we create a pecking order. The call of Jesus to discipleship has been cast by the church into novitiate and seminary callings that now seem too narrow a framework for the gospel call to radical Christianity. Jesus said the commandments were enough for salvation, but not enough for discipleship. It is the challenge to every Christian, and it cuts through every status claim.

We would like to think it is the church itself that is calling us to repent of our sins of sexism, but how can a patriarchal church call itself to leave behind its male dominance? The oppressor may indeed have clues about the feelings of the oppressed, but it is only the oppressed who have the primary experience out of which change can come. The male church can only react. We hope the reaction will be toward identifying with the hurting people and responding in a new way to insights received vicariously. The initiative for change must come from Catholic women. It will come from them without their seeing themselves as feminists because they are part of a culture that embodies their every waking moment. It is the Women's Movement of which Catholic women are a part that is tolling the bell calling women to challenge the male establishments. Pat Mische, a mother and lecturer, sounds the call:

> It is not a question of whether or not there will be altar girls or women priests or even what percentage will be women. These changes will come because the tide of history will be too strong, even for the Catholic Church, to hold out against it for more than one or two more decades. The old logic and old belief systems that support sexual discrimination in the world—which are the same logic and beliefs that support militarism, environmental destruction, and human rights violations—are crumbling every day. The church, as it has in the past, will adapt itself to the imperatives of the new era that is emerging in history, or history will leave it behind. Ultimately, there is still too much wisdom in the church for such a betrayal of its larger purpose and vision.
>
> The deeper impact of the Women's Movement on the church—far deeper than the issue of women's ordination—is that in raising the "women's question," it is ultimately raising questions of power, authority, hierarchical structures and the participation of the laity. In becoming aware of the injustices to women in the church, one becomes sensitized to the larger question of injustice and dehumanization that affects not only women but male priests and all the laity—male as well as female.[2]

A friend confided that it was the display of power in the TV coverage of the two papal deaths and installations that converted her to her present feminist position in the Catholic church. What happens to a sensitive woman whose life has been deeply etched in a Philadelphia Catholic culture and watches with a mother's eyes the phalanxes of white- and red-robed men with peaked hats that make short men larger than life as they parade almost endlessly through the colonnades to the papal altar, where they form a buffer zone between the women and the papal altar? The musicians, servers, lectors, and Communion ministers tell the male story of whose church it is, who defines its doctrines, proclaims its moral positions, and assigns its bishops. What is this saying to her daughter?

It is also a message to the growing cadre of American bishops who would like the church to move to an American version of the heavenly banquet. Sensitive males reject our present clerical and macho symbolic definition of church. A young priest commented after the funeral of Cardinal Cody, which was not different from a papal Mass: "I stood outside of the Cathedral on the corner of Superior and State Streets and enjoyed every moment of the pageantry, but it is not the church to which I belong."

I am "sounding brass and a tinkling cymbal" unless I translate my words into deeds. At the parish Mass celebrating my fortieth anniversary of priesthood I was concerned about the kind of church that would be perceived through the procession and the distribution of people at the altar by role, age, and sex. The ten people in the procession were equally divided according to sex: the age range was thirteen through seventy-one. To make this possible I asked priest friends not to vest and to sit with the people. Vestments root us in our tradition, but too many heavily vested people tell us too much about the past and too little about the present and future.

The first two girls to serve Mass at St. Victor's were daughters of parents who are deeply involved in the ministries of the parish. It is significant that each family had four girls and no boys. It reminded me of a Lutheran minster speaking at a conference on the ordination of women; he said he had a vested interest in the subject because he wanted ordination to be an option for his daughters.

The parishioners in this blue-collar parish are delighted to see their daughters at the altar. The stories are illuminating. After I recessed with a girl server at a funeral Mass I saw an elderly man call the girl aside and whisper to her, "I'm not from this parish. You're the first girl server I've ever seen. I like it." After a Sunday liturgy a visitor approached the pastor to tell him how she was moved to tears at the sight of a girl at the altar. As a child she had cried in bed because she could not serve. While boys and girls serving Mass may trigger warm feelings about our childhood, St. Victor's has yet to make the role of server inclusive of all ages. This will happen when grandmothers and grandfathers serve with their grandsons and granddaughters, and when the single adult, divorced, and widowed take their turn at the altar.

Ushers are greeters. The major concern of the usher should be to welcome people, help them to find a seat, and serve their personal needs so as to facilitate their worship and exemplify that the Lord comes to us in relationships. We would find it strange to enter a restaurant to have only men as the greeters whose role it is to make us feel welcome and comfortable. The response of the male ushers and parishioners to women was immediate and affirmative. Women servers and women ushers are not a test of our faith but of our humanity. Since our parishioners are richly human, they delight in the humanness of seeing both sexes serving in tandem.

Language is the bearer of our culture. It carries with it the marks of an unquestioned tradition that is embedded in our liturgy, Scriptures, and theology—a tradition that for women today is increasingly experienced as subordination and oppression. The fact that the Scriptures and liturgy are texts that the church does not permit us to change forms a double bind. When I pray in public, I find myself changing *he* and *him* to *we* and *us* as I look ahead at the next line. My theological principle in making these minor changes stems from an ancient pastoral principle I learned in a pre-Vatican II seminary. It is called pastoral compassion or, in Greek, *epikeia:* When in doubt, favor compassion. It flows from the New Testament stories of Jesus breaking man-made (and I do mean *man*-made) rules in favor of feeding hungry people. I would rather break a rule than turn off over half the congregation by an oppressive use of pronouns.

If women have not already stopped reading this book because of my frequent references to the kingdom, I am inserting a parenthesis for them. While the kingdom is a basic gospel image that I find necessary to convey the teaching of Jesus, I am aware that it is a male power image that carries more freight than Jesus intended. A king can dominate, oppress, or be paternalistically benign. A king is not only a model of domination but is exclusively male. While we often use *man* as a translation of a Latin word that covers male and female, *king* is exclusively and irrevocably male. Our icons presented Jesus as a regal figure, which supported our church's male hierarchical structures.

As we who are the church move toward identifying with the poor and toward more democratic structures, we will move toward imaging Jesus as the suffering servant of Isaiah. I must leave it to the reader to adapt the Bible's kingly language. I would be untrue to the gospel if I omitted the kingdom concept. Nevertheless, the kingly imagery of the New Testament needs to be juxtaposed with an understanding of Jesus as a sensual and sexual being who broke through his culture and related to women as equals, an aspect of the gospel that has been lost on the church. Sebastian Moore's comments on Jesus' sexuality are incisive:

> He appears to be comfortable with his sexuality in a way that sharply distinguishes him from the conventional image of the holy man of his time. In that very patriarchal society, the holy man kept himself aloof from women. Jesus, apparently, openly enjoyed the company of women and treated them as equals—which men have still not learned to do. This was remarked on, and gave offence. One's image of Jesus is of a man with women around him on an equal footing with men.[3]

Until recently, interpreting the Bible has been the exclusive possession of male theologians, Scripture scholars, and popes. Given the length of time needed to acquire the academic credentials, this is rapidly changing in Catholic and Protestant schools of theology. For example, two of the professors of Scripture at Catholic Theological School in Chicago are women. A corner has been turned.

St. Ann's, the Northeastern University student parish, is my downtown Boston hotel. I joined the community for morning prayers. Sister Joanne, a staff minister, sat at the presider's chair inside the sanctuary, facing the Scriptures. Two young women in jeans were standing on the side opposite me as instrumentalist and cantor. Three women, one of them an elderly parishioner, and I were in the choir stall.

With a woman presiding, I had the good feeling of being out of my familiar male, clerical institution. This was not today's typical Roman Catholic community; this was a New Testament community, where the emphasis was not on the ordained cleric but on the true leader. She was authenticated by her charism as a leader of prayer—a charism evident in her sense of presence and the deliberateness with which she read the prayers.

The evening before, I had been reading the Genesis story of creation. Adam was created an undifferentiated person who did not know what it was to be male until the Adamic personhood was halved and Adam experienced himself as male in the presence of a woman. It was starkly clear that morning that both Sister Joanne and I were priests, however differentiated by sex and ordination.

I decided to find out how important my clerical garb was to my parishioners by wearing a suit and tie to St. Victor's Booster's Club New Year's party. Since it was not a full-blown parish event, the price of nonacceptance by the party-goers was a gamble I could afford. The result was that I felt in touch with my humanity because the party-goers accepted me as a person rather than as a church functionary. I upped the ante and did the same at Victor Elegance, the formal parish dinner dance. Again the affirming posture of parishioners assured me that the basic pastoral relationship of priest and parishioner is a human one.

The primitive instinct of the parishioners is "Does he care for me as a person?" Is he willing to share his life with me, however thin the slice, as one of us? Does he have to meet us in his role even in our fun times? I felt that parishioners and I were closer to the Lord that evening because we had removed one more barrier to sharing our common humanity and building community. The Lord is found in the simple enjoyment of one another's presence as he is in the crisis moments of life. The prophetic message is more easily grasped when it comes from a prophet who is comfortable sharing the joys of life with people rather than standing aloof like Moses holding above them the commandments cut in stone tablets.

The Roman collar at a party has become for me a symbol of separation, a symbol of male, clerical oppression. I continue to wear my clerical garb on Sunday and at wakes, weddings, and other liturgical or quasi-liturgical services as I wear a vestment to help the worshiper link the present service with the twenty-century-old tradition from which we draw our energies.

The clerical garb dramatizes the schizophrenia in the Catholic church. However, in spite of our patriarchal Judeo-Christian history, we can evoke the Scriptures to reinterpret our image of God as embodying both motherly and fatherly qualities. A female monk, Julian of Norwich (d. 1442), who lived outside the walls of St. Julian's Church in Norwich, England, is one of the medieval mystics who is helping us recover our heritage.

> The underlying concern of Julian is that of the totality. What she develops is not the idea of femininity as opposed to or distinct from that of masculinity, but that of the motherhood of God as complement to that of his fatherhood. She does not introduce in her approach to God the vocabulary and the symbolism of sex, which according to its very etymology means a section, a part, a division, the opposite of a totality. She conceives the quality of a mother as present in the Trinity, as well as that of a Father, a Son and their Spirit. It is the plenitude of life, of love, which is proper to each of them and common to the three of them as a unity of the same substance. . . . In no way does she wish to substitute the idea of motherhood of God for that of his fatherhood; she wants to unite them. She works for an integration of all that is best of what we can conceive and experience of God.[4]

We have a patriarchal interpretation of the Scriptures because the interpreters of our culture and of the Scriptures were male hierarchs. By the sheer weight of modern culture, though, the church will be forced to come to terms with God's femininity and motherliness. The deep-sea diving for these scriptural pearls is already in a process that cannot be reversed.

There is the case of the motherly image attributed to God by Isaiah when he wrote: "Like a son comforted by his mother, will I comfort you," and that attributed to Jesus by him when he said: "O Jerusalem! Jerusalem! How often have I longed to gather your children as a hen gathers her brood under her wings." There is also the allusion to "the Father's loving breasts" and to the "milk of the Father" in Clement of Alexandria and to the Spirit as feminine in the time of St. Irenaeus. In the 12th century several Cistercian authors made use of maternal imagery to speak not only of male authority figures, but of God and of "Mother Jesus" as a symbol of tenderness and of supportive love.[5]

If the focus of the church is on the Risen Lord in whose presence we live, rather than on the historical Jesus, we will see Jesus as a universal person who is neither male or female, Irish or Polish, rich or poor. The image of the Risen Lord is not only the antithesis of sexism, racism, and classism, but it opens up a vision of who we can become.

It is easy to fault an insensitive church and not celebrate its inclusion of women in its ministries. While women will continue to clean the church and bake for church sales, women are also acquiring theological and ministerial skills at theology schools, Catholic colleges, and diocesan and parish seminars and workshops. One of the obstacles to this forward movement will be authoritarian and chauvinistic priests, young and old. In parishes without enlightened and understanding priests we cannot expect mature women under thirty to be active members. If the parish has a school, the parents may retain their membership until the last child has graduated. Surprisingly enough, parents will pay a high price to give their children the same Catholic education they received in a church of which they have fond memories but which now they no longer need to tolerate.

On the other hand, parishes that open their ministries to women, include women in full-time staff positions, and have a collegial style of decision-making will be energizing places for both men and women. Within the built-in structural rigidities of an ancient church, a parish can be a sign of the kingdom where men and women feast at the one banquet table.

How can a parish hear itself talk about women's concerns? Archbishop Weakland of Milwaukee asked himself the same question, but on a diocesan scale. He wanted both to find out what women thought and felt about their acceptance as women in their parishes and to discover the wider concerns of women. But he also asked for recommendations to facilitate change. He convened nine women and one man as a special "Task Force on the Role of Women in the Church of Southeastern Wisconsin." After twenty months of dialogue they presented a detailed report that was published in the diocesan paper. A scaled-down model for a parish would seem eminently possible. The following excerpt exemplifies the report's practicality and reinforces the insights of this chapter.

> Whereas no women spoke of their Church's hesitation to receive domestic and nurturing kinds of service, the Task Force heard that when women come forward to offer ideas, insight and experience for decision-making, their contributions are not always met with the same enthusiasm. Women whose experience and education qualify them to run households and/or hold responsible positions in society are increasingly impatient when they are [considered] incompetent until they prove themselves otherwise. A male voice on committee or council, in most cases, still carries more weight than does a female voice, even when they are speaking the same thing. Several specific instances of this were described to the Task Force. In many cases, it seems, women are expected to make coffee while men make decisions. Women who do not abide by that expectation are frequently criticized by men and women alike.[6]

An effective way for the church to get in touch with the issue would be for someone to write and produce a parish, diocesan, or papal version of the movie *Tootsie,* a film that tried to capture the indignities that men inflict on a woman in work life. A Dustin Hoffman as Sister Dorothy Michaels, the parish coordinator or secretary, could dramatize the problem of living up to the ideal that "in [the church of] Jesus Christ there is neither male nor female." However, despite its simple and humorous device of having a man simulate a woman in a way that reveals male domination, *Tootsie* leaves much to be desired. While it points up that a woman's identity at work depends upon, is subject to, and is subordinate to the male establishment, the film reinforces what at first glance it seems to be effectively ridiculing: The male producer of the picture betrays himself as a modern patriarch by using a male actor to define a woman's role in society.

Tootsie is a step forward in helping men to see the pain a woman encounters in living to please men, but we need a film written and directed by a woman that allows the woman to tell the story and share her male-inflicted wounds. Not until males are emotionally vulnerable will they grasp the wisdom of men and women listening to the gospel from the viewpoint of each other's sexuality.

11

A Place for Dissent in the Church

The bishops' pastoral on peace and nuclear arms, entitled *The Challenge of Peace: God's Promise and Our Response,* set off a Fourth of July fireworks display in the church, but not everyone saw it as a Declaration of Independence freeing us from servitude to our government-military-industrial complex. Instead, many educated and influential Catholics saw themselves as being oppressed by a hierarchy that is speaking to lay issues without their advice and consent.

Hackles are always raised when a church enters a political dialogue with more than prayerful restatements of tired appeals to unity and the common good. At times the hue and cry is from someone whose ox is being gored: a Catholic grower enraged at bishops supporting his migrant workers' quest for union representation, or a Catholic government official crying "Foul!" from a Pentagon window. But if the bishops had not spoken out, the church historians would have grouped them with the German bishops and the pope who did not speak out forcefully against the Holocaust—churchmen who were more interested in protecting the rights of the church than expressing rage at the herding of millions of Jews into the gas chambers of Dachau and Auschwitz.

Abigail McCarthy writes:

How best can the church exercise her prophetic role? "There is something to be said for a church in which authority does not come from the grass roots; grass roots are sometimes poisoned," wrote Brogan in 1956 apropos of the American bishops' then strengthening stand against racism. . . .

Today at long last, the church espouses with a clear voice the cause of the poor and the oppressed, and the question of human rights would seem as compelling as the problems of racism and Nazism. Mindful of the independence of the Catholic citizen, mindful of the past (perhaps still lingering) distrust of the church in the arena of foreign policy, should the church not seek concrete solutions for complicated problems with the help of those whose responsibility those problems are or have been?[1]

It is certainly true that people welcome a prophetic voice that cries out for the rights of billions of people in a world that lacks a unified voice speaking on behalf of humanity. The Catholic church, with its worldwide constituency, its centralized authority structures, and its office of papacy, can speak to world leaders on behalf of human rights. Regional and national hierarchies can speak for human rights with the tongue and metaphor of the people, and with more specificity. However, the question we are raising in this chapter is, when an articulate leadership speaks for, but apart from, its members, what effect does that have on the development of the gifts and leadership of those members? Does this bring about two churches: the church teaching and speaking on political issues, and the church as the people who are immersed in these issues as their lay calling? One question suggests another: What style of leadership is most effective in calling forth and developing the gifts of the gathered community? The question raised in this chapter flows from a church leadership that speaks to sensitive issues that touch people's lives: What are the styles and perimeters of dissent?

Charism and church establishment are the two poles of a tension that is characteristic of the Catholic church. The balance tilts from one side to the other as the Body of Christ winds its way through cultural change. The New Testament church was a church of marginalized groups held together by traveling apostles who took up collections for the needy and helped the people clarify and develop their understandings of Jesus' message. Its members ministered to one another according to their gifts. Ordination was not a part of the vocabulary of the people of the Way.

As the church grew and ministries or charisms got out of hand—in the church of Corinth, for instance—order was introduced. Ordination became increasingly significant. The balance shifted to the side of those gifted with authority, the authority conferred by the rite of ordination. Ministry was taken over by the ordained. The Reformation was a revolt against the oppression of the people through the clericalization of authority in the church. We are still trying to keep alive charism, which Scripture says "blows where it will," and the necessary structure that ordination imposes on the charism of leadership.

Except in Scripture readings, the word *ministry* almost disappeared in the Catholic church until the middle of this century, when new forces tried to tilt the church toward the charismatic or the small group.

In the Latin American church of this century, the charismatic church is on the rise through the hundreds of thousands of basic communities (in Spanish, *comunidades de base*) that have sprung up like wild flowers across the continent. Under the leadership of Cardinal Arns of Sao Paulo, Brazil, a significant number of the hierarchy helped give shape and form to the fresh understandings of Christianity arising from small groups that have filtered their experience of poverty and oppression through the biblical images and have met the Lord in the reality of their situation. Here was an example of a strong, hierarchical leadership in a living and creative tension with people who were in touch with the Lord under conditions that were a stench to the nostrils of God. Like artful dancers they found each other's rhythm.

Professor Robert Bellah, a sociologist of religion and a Protestant, nevertheless warns us about being seduced by the Latin American basic communities.

The valid self-criticism following Vatican II may have obscured the importance of the church model for some Catholics. The recent emphasis on small, egalitarian base communities centering on the Eucharist has its value; but as an exclusive emphasis these base communities could easily repeat the errors of Protestant sectarianism—they would end by reinforcing privatization and depoliticization rather than combating them. I think only the church type has a chance to combat effectively the self-destructive tendencies of modern society, and I would say that to fellow Protestants, who have never completely abandoned the church model, as well as to Catholics.[2]

While Bellah's commentary may keep us from romanticizing, the North American Catholic church is light years away from approximating the Latin American model. Indeed, the American church needs to look to its own history, rather than to Latin America, to develop its own style of leadership that maximizes the gifts of all.

The American church, with its own identity flowing from the American experience, came into being with Bishop John Carroll's election as its first bishop. The first four bishops were *elected* by the priests in the colonies. Moreover, lay people were in control of parish finances. But the American church began to lose its homegrown democratic character when the bishops panicked in 1844 and took away control of the purse strings from the parish trustees and gave total control to the pastor. Vatican I in 1870 was an effort to centralize Vatican authority more tightly. But in protecting orthodoxy it was stifling charisms. In 1892 Cardinal Gibbons did his best to suppress covertly the Second Lay Congress that was held in Chicago in 1893. Ironically, the American church would experience gospel freedom only after it had belatedly accepted much of Western Europe's anti-church Enlightenment movement.[3]

Vatican II sought to redress the imbalance wrought by Vatican I. For the Roman curia, one of the first upsetting events was African hierarchies meeting at Vatican II without prior permission. This could mean block voting and cutting the strings that had them tied to Rome in such a way that they had not been able to discuss issues and develop indigenous churches.

The American hierarchy, though with much timidity, also began to feel themselves to be a body that shared a common experience and had its own way of reflecting on life, the gospel, and church.

Father John Courtney Murray, who was considered to be an embarrassment to the American hierarchy during the first session, became its hero in the final session by contributing his American experience of religious liberty to a universal church that believed that one had to become a Catholic to authentically experience God's saving word. The identity of the American bishops as leaders of an American church that is Catholic rather than Roman continues to grow. Its finest hour was in November of 1982 at its annual meeting at the Capital Hilton in Washington, D.C. The final passage of the pastoral on May 3, 1983, at the Chicago Palmer House was the denouement. This 45,000-word document, with its carefully reasoned and delicately nuanced distinctions, became the American church teaching on peace in an era threatened by nuclear warfare.

The question we are raising in this chapter is, How can Catholics who disagree with the church's teaching continue to be Catholics in good standing, that is, not living in sin? As the pastoral letter weaves through the subtleties of many-faceted moral issues, it attempts to make clear that not all its statements have the same moral authority:

> We address many concrete questions concerning the arms race, contemporary warfare, weapons systems and negotiating strategies. We do not intend that our treatment of each of these issues carry the same moral authority as our statement of universal moral principles and formal church teaching. . . . When making application of these principles we realize—and we wish readers to recognize—that prudential judgments are involved based on specific circumstances which can change or which can be interpreted differently by people of good will (e.g., the treatment of "no first use"). We shall do our best to indicate, stylistically and substantively, whenever we make such applications.[4]

The bishops as our moral leaders may give us the perimeters of a document's binding force, but it is the faith-filled Catholic people, the church, that will ultimately ratify the document or consign it to the archives under the heading of "Documents That Never Took Hold."

In preparing the peace pastoral, the bishops over a period of twenty-two months consulted the faithful as well as segments of the scientific, military, and government worlds, and in the process developed three drafts that were submitted to the membership for suggestions. It is a landmark and model for the consultative process for future church documents. The process may prove to be more important than the finished product. While the consultation process and the bishops' astute performance on TV screens throughout the world cannot be faulted, the document, signed and sealed by the bishops as the official teaching of the American church, must be ratified by the people. It may take the rest of the century to know which parts of the pastoral have been accepted and which have been rejected.

Pope Leo XIII's papal letter "On the Condition of Labor" issued in 1891 illustrates our point. At its promulgation it was widely perceived as a radical church document, branded as socialist, and not accepted in many church quarters because it claimed for working people the right to free association. It was a ringing endorsement of labor unions. Ratification came in this country in the late thirties, when unions were accepted by the people in the New Deal era. Half a century after the papal letter, the prophetic insight had become conventional wisdom. If a Gallup poll majority had been the criterion for ratification, the letter clearly would have failed. Prophecy or church teaching must have the staying power of decades to be of God. Other papal documents issued with the same papal authority were quickly relegated to the circular file. Vatican II documents had the same unevenness of acceptance. The *Dogmatic Constitution on the Church* and the *Pastoral Constitution on the Church in the Modern World* are today reference points in church teaching. They continue to be ratified by the holdouts of an earlier generation and at the same time are a starting place for the new. Many other Vatican II documents are seldom used as reference points for Catholic teaching.

In a perceptive article Andrew Greeley argues that Catholics will continue to be practicing Catholics and yet will dissent from significant church teaching without cynicism or guilt. While his study is based on young people's response to church sexual teaching, his conclusions apply to the peace pastoral and other authoritative church pronouncements:

> There are two major and glacial shifts that the data seems to indicate: 1) an appeal from the institutional church leadership to God and 2) a conviction that God does not want you to stay away from church because you reject a specific teaching of the church. The devout dissidents are rejecting any claim by the magisterium to have a monopoly on God.[5]

In the post-peace-pastoral church the hawks and the doves will continue to share the same bread and drink from the same cup, but the tension will remain. The prophecy that moved from *The Catholic Worker* pacifism of the thirties, the Berrigan-inspired symbolic destructive actions, the pacifist writings of Thomas Merton, and the Pax Christi pacifist cell within the bishops' own ranks is now embedded in the hierarchical structure of the church. The Washington Capital Hilton became for some the national shrine and sign of the prophetic American and Roman church much as the National Shrine of the Immaculate Conception in Washington D.C., is the shrine and sign of the devotional American immigrant church. Whether the tension proves creative or destructive will unfold on the screen of history. That a single prophetic document makes a prophetic or peace church seems too large a claim.

The peace pastoral set up a countervailing force of lay Catholic intellectuals, scholars, pundits, and government officials who see the hierarchy speaking for them in areas in which the hierarchy does not have the special competencies that people in the pews have. New Catholic lay groups were formed that initially excluded clergy and religious from leadership roles.

This tension was expressed in the widely publicized 1977 *Chicago Declaration of Christian Concern*. The signers were concerned with the takeover by the clergy of social action initiatives, the disappearance of Catholic Action-inspired lay groups, the clergy's preoccupation with housekeeping chores, and the narrowing of the word *ministry* to liturgical and teaching ministries. The Declaration speaks for the wider constituency of a loyal opposition remaining in the church and at the same time critiquing it.

But another segment of disaffected educated lay Catholics known as "Communal Catholics" quietly slipped out of the church. To them, the enemy was the "institutional church," an authoritarian church that no longer spoke to their experience in the secular world. They left more from boredom and a conviction that the church was irrelevant than from anger. They had found no place for themselves in what they perceived as a clergy-dominated church. They had seen churchmen playing religious games that no longer spoke to life.

Yet another group, the neo-orthodox lay intellectuals, seem to be calling for a church with a House of Lords and a House of Commons. By highlighting the clergy-lay distinction they are not simply asking for a balance of power but for a separation of sacred and secular roles. While the American Catholic experience has seesawed from an eighteenth-century congregational style to a more hierarchically controlled immigrant church, the two-tiered church these neo-orthodox lay intellectuals are calling for is neither the universal experience nor the American Catholic experience.

Gregory Baum in responding to the *Chicago Declaration of Christian Concern* writes:

> The social movements in the Church and the significant conflicts associated with them pass right through clergy and laity. Let me give a simple example. The effort of Hispanic Americans, most of whom are Catholics, for a self-confident cultural identity and public recognition of their collectivity involves many people and provokes many responses, in the Church and outside the Church, but nowhere is the simple clergy-laity distinction a useful conceptual tool for understanding the social phenomenon.[6]

The church's present self-understanding of church is not an over/against, clergy/laity model. The pronouncements or pastoral statements of the official church do not evoke pavlovian responses from the people. The bishops have learned this from the birth control and abortion issues, and it extends to such doctrinal issues as papal infallibility. The only way the official church documents can be teaching instruments is through a style in which their statements and decrees are a response to an intense listening process. To be accepted, a church document must be filtered through the religious experience of the people.

Sensitivity to human experience does not mean that bishops should follow the Gallup polls and offer a majority position to Catholics. But the prophetic statement, which by definition is a minority stance, must be a respectful response to grassroots listening. One need not be accused of aristocratic arrogance to believe that the roots can be poisoned. Those outside church officialdom, not to be equated with "laity," are developing forums that pull together their religious experience as biblically oriented American Catholics. Indeed this is happening and is an evident strength of the American church. The evidences are in the print media, professional associations, and independent advocacy groups.

For example, the *National Catholic Reporter*, which has a modest circulation of 50,000, is a bellwether for reporting on the official church and the church in the world. While it is published and edited by lay people, its board of directors includes priests and religious who represent a large percentage of readers and supporters. Week after week, sensitive and controversial pastoral and theological issues are raised in a format that allows for a variety of perspectives not allowed in diocesan papers. Bishops take off their mitres while reading it and take seriously its insights about the church in the world and the critiques of their own behavior as a part of officialdom.

Commonweal, a sixty-year-old weekly edited by Catholic lay persons, has nourished generations of Catholic intellectuals, known prior to Vatican II as *Commonweal* Catholics. While its writers and subscribers are overwhelmingly lay, it has published articles by priests and bishops. It challenged the church's complicity with the Franco fascist government in the thirties and together with *The Catholic Worker* openly opposed Cardinal Spellman in the gravedigger strike in the forties.

Catholicism in Crisis: A Journal of Lay Catholic Opinion (Jacques Maritain Center, Notre Dame) is a 1980s response of lay Catholic intellectuals to the American hierarchy's confronting our government in economic, political, and social issues. It both questions the bishops' analyses and would restrict the role of bishops in addressing the public order. The editorial board includes names of Catholic scholars who are also associated with ecumenical journals that critique church leaders.

The Wanderer, an independent Catholic weekly, has been a catalyst in articulating for a wide audience the concerns of Catholics who feel that a tiny but influential group of theologians and bishops have misled the faithful by the way in which they have interpreted the fundamentals of the Catholic church. *Twin Circle* and other publications often oppose the stance espoused by the *National Catholic Reporter,* the United States Catholic Conference, and the official Catholic Press.

Crosscurrents is a Catholic scholarly quarterly edited by lay Catholic academicians. It specializes in European and Latin American translations of philosophical and theological articles not otherwise available.

Meanwhile, to look briefly at professional associations, we note that Catholic biblical scholars and theologians, taking their cue from Pius XII in 1942, no longer look to Rome for instructions on how to think and what to write. They have developed in their disciplines through membership in the wider biblical and theological communities as well as within their own American associations.

Diocesan and parochial structures are slower to respond to the breakthroughs in religious experiences of the people they represent and the developments in the Catholic intellectual community. "Dominant structures have always been conformist in regard to their culture," writes Baum. "I don't expect a revolution from the top." He prefers working outside the church structures rather than spending his energies in reforming them. "I want to promote renewal movements—re-thinking and renewing Christianity, in small groups. There is an endless variety of them: religious, sisters, brothers, lay people, minority groups, women, Asians, and so forth. There is great vitality there, even though it is not mainstream."[7]

I have written this book because I believe that the church at the parish level has greater potential than my colleague

Gregory Baum admits for being a prophetic voice in a neighborhood, territorial parish. Although it has restraints laid upon it, it has access to all levels of the church bureaucracy to plead the cause of the disenfranchised and poor for all local communities.

Besides Catholic publications that are not dependent financially upon the church institution, and besides a lively and Catholic intellectual community that exercises its academic freedom, there is need for national and local advocacy groups that can watchdog the local and universal church and call it to accountability. If the Catholic church, which is perceived as authoritarian in its leadership structures, does not have channels for dissent, truth will be muted and creativeness will be buried.

Dissent in the church has been a part of our apostolic tradition. The tradition began with Paul confronting Peter to his face about Peter's refusal to admit Gentiles to The Way without the rite of circumcision. Catherine of Siena has been honored for her jawboning the popes for living in exile in sunny France. Thomas More stood up against the English bishops by being ready to accept death rather than betray the church.

In 1974 the American bishops called for a national consultation process to surface concerns by holding hearings locally and bringing them to a national forum for discussion and action. The final convocation of Call to Action was held in Cobo Hall, Detroit. The experience was less successful than the planners and participants had anticipated, and the mixed results discouraged further attempts. The need of finances and a staff to organize a similar conference without episcopal sponsorship seems to prohibit an unofficial group from undertaking such a project.

The Association of Rights for Catholics in the Church was launched in Europe the day after the Vatican censured the Swiss theologian Hans Küng. It is forming national and local chapters in an effort to develop a charter for rights of Catholics. One model for such a charter is the United Nations Charter of Human Rights. It would be unrealistic to perceive the new code of church law drafted by the official church as adequate, given the reality that it was drafted without consultation with local congregations, minorities, and subcultures.

The Chicago Call to Action offers a model of an independent activist group that works outside the official Catholic structures but within the church of Chicago. Resigned priests and their wives, veterans of the Christian Family Movement, young peace activists, and a few priests form the leadership that is able to raise issues that cut across all segments of the church and yet may be too embarrassing for church officials to raise. Such a group offers a healthy counterpoint to the authority figures in the church. At the same time, a strong episcopal leadership is necessary for a fruitful tension with the special-interest groups within the household. The leadership needs to take firm positions and be willing to dialogue with equally strong groups who hold different views. Such persons, in the jargon of the eighties, are "process persons."

The Association of Chicago Priests is an independent association of priests, which to many priests is an anomaly. But the members believe that within their promise of obedience to the bishop in the rite of ordination they retain the natural right of freedom of assembly and the right to pursue professional interests without prior authorization by their bishop. This Association offers a model for priests who see it as a professional response to priestly ministry.

While some may feel that the bishops are speaking too forcefully for the church and equate church with themselves, the reality is that the church is becoming laicized without ceasing to be hierarchical. The shift revolves around ministry. *Ministry* is a New Testament word that has no necessary relationship to ordination. In the apostolic church people named, claimed, and later were empowered to use their gifts in the name of the community. As the church became clericalized, these ministries were swallowed up by priesthood. This direction reversed itself in the seventies, with *ministry* becoming again a generic term that includes both the ordained and the nonordained. Coleman writes:

> The adoption of "ministry" language has gradually shifted
> several important priorities in possession a decade ago.
> For example, the appeal to the language of ministry assumes that baptism takes priority of eminence over or-

dination. . . . To speak of ministry is to evoke this whole gestalt of the priority of baptism, charism, competence and collegiality over ordination, office, status and hierarchy. . . . It is precisely and increasingly priesthood that seems a residual category whose essence is difficult to discern.[8]

The shift is bringing new tensions into the local church. Old diocesan and parish structures are being tested. New wine is being poured into old wineskins that must burst. An enlightened style of leadership by bishops and pastors is needed as charisms are being tested. The challenge offers new possibilities for those called to prophecy. In the whole history of the post-apostolic age there has never been a better climate than the present for prophetic parishes to renew society.

12

Wrestling with Our Own Demons

Conversion is not a single event but a process, a journey with twists and turns, a journey on which we lose our way and find it again. It is a trail of peaks and valleys, joyous celebrations and bouts of despair, sudden insights and dark nights of the soul. It is not a call to be successful in implementing the dream but to be faithful. The overriding goal of the parish is to facilitate the conversion process for people.

Until recent decades a devout Lutheran or a biblically oriented Baptist entering the Roman Catholic church was called a convert. Since we did not trust Protestants' belief in Jesus Christ, we baptized these people conditionally. Today we trust the faith of other Christians who are baptized in the same Lord Jesus; however, we no longer refer to them as converts, but rather as persons who have changed their religious affiliation through reception into full communion with the Catholic church. Conversion now means the inner process of turning to the Lord Jesus as Savior.

Conversion in the biblical sense is turning to the Lord with one's whole soul, mind, and body. When the Lord says to us, "Repent, the kingdom of God is at hand," he is calling us to turn from our selfish ways and accept him as our sovereign Lord to whom we have been committed through baptism. Conversion captures in one word two of the words used frequently by Jesus in his preaching: *repent* and *kingdom*.

Evangelist Jim Wallis writes and preaches about Jesus' calling us to turn away from anything that stands in the way of our identifying with the kingdom.[1] What makes Jim different from many other evangelicals and from many contemporary Catholics is that he names the demons in our culture. He makes it clear that by failing to name the demons, we worship the demonic and are a party to social sin. He spells out conversion as our responding to the call of Jesus to commit ourselves to him as Lord and Savior. This commitment means naming the demons we have allowed to dominate our lives and acknowledging the power we have given those demons; without this there is no reconciliation. Jim's naming of demons such as militarism, racism, and sexism sets him apart from preachers who prefer to stay with the gospel of self-improvement. The axis of life, according to that gospel, is a narcissistic self-centeredness rather than a God-centered self that reaches out to our neighbor in a personal, individual caring way as well as to our neighbor in relation to the infrastructures of society that determine our way of life.

Naming the demonic in our social system raises a hue and cry from the American Catholic who denies complicity with the system. Including social sin in our preaching represents an immense change in American Catholicism.

The American liberal tradition, which mainline Protestant and Catholics alike have accepted as an authentic carrier of the gospel, does not acknowledge social sin. It sees nothing wrong with the American society that social engineering cannot remedy. Our country was put back on course after the Depression, World War II, Vietnam, and Watergate. The American people are still reluctant to admit there is anything wrong with our society that more expertise in research and planning, a more efficient crime detection and penal system, and an improved educational process, will not solve. Even when we incisively question our belief in democracy, psychology, the physical sciences, and technology, we are still adamant as a people in believing it will all come together again without an acknowledgment and confession of our guilt.

The radical left of the sixties, who did not accept conversion as the ingredient for real change in our society, left the scene long before the liberals began to feel unsure. Jerry Rubin, former Yippy, no longer able to deal with his fears and anxieties, turned to the West Coast spiritual supermarkets to shore up his sagging ego rather than to the Lord to repent and enter the kingdom. Rubin says that in five years, he directly experienced est, gestalt therapy, bioenergetics, rolfing, massage, jogging, health foods, tai chi, Esalen, hypnotism, modern dance, meditation, Silva Mind control, Arica, acupuncture, sex therapy, Reichian therapy, and More House—a smorgasbord course in New Consciousness.

The radical Catholic tradition, or the Catholic left, has its roots in the Catholic Worker movement, ACTU (American Catholic Trade Unionists), the Catholic peace movement, and the Catholic Action movement of the fifties. This Catholic left challenged Catholics to see their work, family, and civic life as the locus of the Spirit. Its theology was rooted in the Pauline teaching of the Mystical Body and was fed by the American liturgical movement that began in the early forties. While it did not use today's language of baptismal commitment, conversion, and kingdom, it had its Catholic Action song, could sing "Solidarity Forever" with the radical left, and later "We Shall Overcome." While it lacked a biblical language and imagery, it spoke to human life in its widest social dimensions without challenging the church's privatized spirituality incarnated in Our Sorrowful Mother novenas. Prior to the middle sixties, like the church of Poland today, it was not interested in challenging church structures. It found adequate freedom in a Vatican I church.

A quarter century after Vatican II, the Catholic left, except for the United Farm Workers, does not exist in the American labor movement, but it is the bearer of the *Catholic Worker* traditions of feeding the poor, sheltering the homeless, finding common cause with the Central American church that has moved to the left in opposition to repressive governments, and is the root of the American peace movement that includes a large segment of the American bishops.

This radical or prophetic wing of the church, tiny but healthy, is challenging the centrist Catholic to look at our social system as the possible cause of our unemployment, our drive for military supremacy, crime in the streets, decaying cities, school systems unable to educate, government agencies tied in bureaucratic knots, middle-income overburdened taxpayers, and an electoral system that sees declining percentages of people voting. Yet this is the social system that has given us what we cherish most in life—homes, freedoms of church and state, a history of openness to immigrants, and generosity abroad.

The left has no counter ideology to present. It simply keeps naming the demons in our society, affirming that there will be no conversion until the demons are called by name and exorcised or driven out.

However, we see our true model in the life of Jesus. After his baptism, he called for repentance and then gave his charter for the New Way in the sermon on the mount. But Matthew and Luke place an important element in the conversion process between the baptism of Jesus and the proclamation of the beatitudes as the norm for Jesus' followers. It was the forty days in the desert, described in Mark's Gospel as the wilderness in which Jesus symbolically wrestled with the wild beasts and the angels.

The conversion process will make no impact on society or be full gospel Christianity until the prospective convert encounters the Lord in the desert and wrestles with the tempter. For the temptations of the Lord parallel our own. He was tempted to manipulate society by calling attention to his own powers. He chose the route of calling people to put aside personal ambition, give way to the sovereign claims of the Father, and let their lives be led and transformed by the power of the Spirit, to choose the cross rather than a bag of tricks. The prison cell has been a wilderness symbol for people who have made a significant difference in human life: Dorothy Day, Eugene Debs, Martin Luther King, Jr., Anwar Sadat, and Mohandas Gandhi. Catholics have tried to structure desert experiences through retreats, Cursillos, and Marriage Encounters in which people, with the support of a community, can wrestle with the Lord. It is always a solitary experience when we enter the wastelands of ourselves and cultivate a contemplative style of prayer that combines the mystic and the activist in one life. It is the kind of prayer modeled by Jesus, who prayed in the desert at night and faced the stupidity of his disciples, the craftiness of his enemies, and the miseries of the poor and helpless during the day. The system that oppressed the poor and debilitated the oppressors was never separated from his prayer to the Father.

In the Catholic tradition the conversion process is a process that takes us through the twists and turns of life rather than the once-and-for-all moment when we experience being saved. While memorable conversion experiences do happen through sudden losses, unexpected gifts of love, or more structured prayer encounters, we see them as markers on a conversion journey that ends only in death. The prophetic parish calls for a conversion spirituality that differs from the devotional spirituality of an immigrant church.

The greatest contribution I can make to the kingdom is not to write a book about the kingdom but to let the kingdom come into my life, to become converted to servanthood. Almost fifty years ago I pronounced the vows of poverty, chastity, and obedience. Today I feel that I have yet to live those vows, to become converted, to die to my selfishness and let the Lord Jesus take over my life.

For decades I prayed each day after Mass that the Lord would take over in my life that day and that I would be clay in the hands of the potter, an instrument of his love. I always felt that by saying these prayers, it would somehow happen. The reality is that conversion does not take place simply by taking vows or saying prayers. Through genuine conversion one becomes an instrument for the Lord to play upon.

The conversion plays itself out in the struggle to let go of my desire to be Number One in competing with the people with whom I work. It is the struggle to let go of my prejudices about particular people in the community who do not agree with me, to let go of my need for approval from the people I have set up as authorities, to let go of my need to build a monument to myself by institutionalizing my work so that I will be remembered after death.

Conversion is the Lord's work, done in the Lord's time. Conversion is the foolishness of David taking on Goliath, Jacob wrestling with the angel, Jesus telling his disciples that the cross is the only way for them as it was for him. Victory comes from losing, from letting go rather than taking charge. It is a bitter pill to swallow that I must die for others in order to live. Conversion is not social engineering but engaging the principalities and powers set on destroying this world. For the

Christian, victory or conversion comes through the daily crucifixion of one's own selfishness.

When Jesus talks about selling all one's possessions, giving to the poor, and following him, or about embracing a way of life that is more difficult than going through the eye of the needle, his hearers are stunned at the impossibility of meeting his challenge. He tells them that what is impossible with mere humans is possible with God. Conversion is the gift we prepare for each day. Through daily struggle we strive to empty ourselves so that the Spirit can fill us. This strikes a blow at believers in the American dream who look back at our history as merely a work of human enterprise and who see its current failure as due to a lack of courage to bring it back to life.

Conversion is another name for self-surrender. In a letter in 1966 to a person deeply involved in the peace movement, Thomas Merton captures both this powerlessness of our actions and our need to act:

> Do not depend on hope of results. When you are doing the sort of work you have taken on, essentially an apostolic work, you may have to face the fact that your work will be apparently worthless and even achieve no result at all, if not perhaps results opposite to what you expect. . . .
>
> The big results are not in your hands or mine, but they suddenly happen, and we can share in them; but there is no point in building our lives on this personal satisfaction, which may be denied us and which after all is not that important. . . . All the good that you will do will not come from you but from the fact that you have allowed yourself, in the obedience of faith, to be used by God's love. . . . If you can get free from the domination of causes and just serve Christ's truth, you will be able to do more and will be less crushed by the inevitable disappointments. The real hope then is not in something we think we can do, but in God who is making something good out of it in some way we cannot see.[2]

Transformation is different from formation. Formation is the lifetime preparation we have had that provides a framework for our decision at moments of transformation. It includes our parental training, our education by school, community, and church, and how we have responded to previous invitations of the Lord. Our response to the Spirit's movement within us does not happen in a vacuum. Formation is the work we do while waiting for the moment when the angel will stir the waters and the man with the withered body who has been waiting at the side of the pool for thirty-eight years can be lifted into the pool (John 5:1-9). The angel who stirs the waters is the transforming agent. The person who lifts the man into the water provides the necessary formation work, without which the angel would not have someone to transform.

Transformation takes place in crisis moments when a decision must be made. It happens when we come to a fork in the road, when we have lost a job, our health, our spouse, our youth, or when we simply know that we cannot continue with our present life no matter how much it has nourished us in the past. The paths that lead in opposite directions stand starkly there before us, and we cannot postpone the decision. Our formation will be the major factor in the choice. Our parental training, our secular and Christian education, the insights of our mentors will all make their claims in this moment of decision. It is the angel stirring the waters. The Lord proposes. We are asked only to surrender, to say yes.

In 1952 Martin Luther King, Jr., had turned down the presidency of the Montgomery NAACP to pursue the scholarly work of finishing his doctoral dissertation and enjoy the rewards of a devoted pastor of souls. A few months later when Rosa Parks refused to go to the back of the bus and the black ministers decided to organize a bus boycott, to Martin's amazement they voted unanimously to make the new minister in town its chairman. It was the Lord calling him to give up the dream of a brilliant career as theologian to take over the role of prophet. Both the formation he had received as the preacher's son and the theological expertise of his university training were the tools the community had given him to put at the service of the transforming call to leave all and follow Jesus.

The Roman Catholic church's official approach to formation is a 1974 document called the Rite of Christian Initiation of

Adults. The opening paragraph captures the spirit of the document. The catechumens "hear the preaching of the mystery of Christ, the Holy Spirit opens their hearts, and they freely and knowingly seek the living God and enter the path of faith and conversion. By God's help, they will be strengthened spiritually in their preparation and at the proper time they will receive the sacraments fruitfully."

It is a clear statement that the church is moving away from a child-centered church toward an adult church where baptism is preceded by a lengthy conversion process. This document is hailed by liturgists as the most revolutionary statement since the agreement of the Council of Jerusalem (circa A.D. 50) in which it was decreed that Gentile converts to The Way would henceforth not be circumcised but simply baptized. The emphasis now is not on the ritual of the sacraments but on the journey of faith that the catechumen enters with the parish, which itself becomes revitalized by the freshness of the gospel as that gospel is received and lived by the neophytes, their sponsors, and the catechumenate team. It links the sacraments to the traditions of the early church.

The Baltimore Catechism with its question-and-answer format was the standard formation tool for American parishes for almost a century. The converts and Catholic and public grade school children handed on the Catholic tradition by memorizing doctrinal statements, accepting the ten commandments and the precepts of the church as guides to morality, and learning Catholic customs such as using holy water and genuflecting before the Blessed Sacrament. The Catechism offered no format for discussing one's images of God or one's experience of the humanity of Jesus. Nor was social sin a category; a KKK could be baptized without being questioned about racism. Under the guise of transmitting the traditions handed down to us from the apostles, we were baptizing the American secular culture that became the wrapper for our baptismal promises. Except for the Legion of Decency film guide we had no way of separating American tribal customs from gospel teaching.

We confused the Catholic subculture with a living faith in the Lord Jesus as Savior. By not relating faith to our culture we blessed the destructiveness in our social institutions. In the

1983 Chicago mayoral election the black candidate received the lowest percentage of votes in the southwest side, which had the city's highest percentage of Catholic population and of Catholic grade and high school graduates. While Catholic parishes and schools in this area, which I once served as high-school teacher and as parish priest, did not overtly promote racism, the absence of formation programs that challenged racism actually aided and abetted parishioners and Catholic school students in living in a sinful situation.

The RCIA offers an educational model that is engaging. It draws people into internalizing Christianity by forming small Christian communities. While the RCIA offers an educational process through which people confront human situations as they reflect on the Scriptures, there is no assurance that it will not perpetuate our secular culture. If the justice message is not at the heart of the Christian message, there is no guarantee that the RCIA will make a difference.

While call, kingdom, and conversion are part of the RCIA vocabulary and are, we hope, becoming part of the Catholic lexicon of the '80s, the question remains: How will the new evangelists speak about demons? The conversion process is always the call to discipleship and to naming the demons that possess us. It is presumed that when we name the demon, the grace or gift of repentance will bring about a conversion.

We pose the following questions to the leaders of the new formation movements: Will the preachers and the catechists name the institutions or structures of our society that oppress people or water down the gospel of Jesus to a psychological or self-improvement appeal to our narcissistic age? Will the conversion be from bad manners to a Christian politeness, or will it follow the lead of Jesus in naming the principalities and powers of darkness? Will the emphasis be on sacramental signs that point to a more intense church life, or will it call people to witness the gospel to a society that equates the kingdom with the rewards of an economic and political system that is the underpinning of a hedonistic, consumerist, militaristic society? Will it be band-aiding, or will it be prophetic? The answers will be determined by the formation of the evangelists. If there is no prophet among the evangelizing team, the RCIA movement is doomed to perpetuate the demonic that is entrenched in our parishes. Again comes our refrain: "Where there is no vision, the people perish."

The prophetic parish must self-consciously plan formation programs that go beyond the catechumenate stage. When I was a high-school teacher and chaplain for Young Christian Students we had study weeks in the summer and annual retreats in the winter. Weekly meetings with a Gospel passage as a centerpiece were not enough. This tiny group of sophomores and juniors taking a prophetic stance over against faculty and students would have been chewed up unless they periodically had left their surroundings to rekindle the fires that were burned out by a counter-culture stance toward one's environment. Since campfires were not part of my culture, I can only fantasize the hypnotic effect they could have upon our imagination and what a community could do to give purpose and resolve to these new images.

The prophetic parish, which depends upon small groups of people to be catalytic agents for the entire parish, must find ways of structuring blocks of time for people to be away from their daily routine to assess and deepen their relationship with the Lord. St. Victor Parish has the luxury of a thirty-room empty convent that has been converted into a parish retreat center called Jubilee House. While Jubilee House is used for retreats for youth groups and for engaged and married couples, the staple of the House is Jubilee Weekends.

These weekends are for men and women who are open to the Spirit descending upon them in the form of tongues of fire. The pastor, Father Leo Mahon, presents the staple biblical themes of God, Jesus, the kingdom, reconciliation, the Eucharist, and the Second Coming. The retreatants are able to pursue in small-group discussion the implications of the related Gospel stories and parables. In the process many experience the Emmaus story of finding a Jesus to whom they can relate; they experience a new understanding of church as community.

It cannot be presumed that retreatants will make the connection between sin and social injustices as easily as they relate sin to sexual deviation. The preaching of the kingdom must be integrated at every level, as opposed to a two-tiered educational model of first private sin and second social sin.

A parish formation program is reinforced by a Sunday parish liturgy that integrates social teaching in its homilies, an inclusiveness in its liturgical ministries, music that is not sentimental, and a presider who offers a celebrative presence. The weekend liturgy is the only formational parish program in which most parishioners participate.

Parishioners need to have resources available for a critical approach to faith development and to church social teaching. Scripture courses and a resource center for books, tapes, and audiovisual materials may be a luxury that no one parish can afford. But clusters of parishes and diocesan facilities can make feasible what is too large an undertaking for one parish.

It is the unending task of the prophetic nucleus in every parish to continue exploring new approaches to raising religious consciousness.

13

The Fire-maker Myth

I have a dream that one day every valley shall be exalted, every hill and mountain shall be made low, the rough places will be made plain, and the crooked places will be made straight, and the glory of the Lord shall be revealed, and all flesh shall see it together.

This is our hope. This is the faith with which I return to the South. With this faith we will be able to hew out of the mountain of despair a stone of hope. With this faith we will be able to transform the jangling discords of our nation into a beautiful symphony of brotherhood. . . .

When we let freedom ring, when we let it ring from every village and every hamlet, from every state and every city, we will be able to speed up that day when all of God's children, black men and white men, Jews and Gentiles, Protestants and Catholics, will be able to join hands and sing in the words of that old Negro spiritual, "Free at last! Free at last! Thank God Almighty, we are free at last!"[1]

I too have a dream—a dream of our parish being aware that it is a sign of God's kingdom to the people in our area and to all the people our parishioners come in contact with through their families, neighborhood, work, and play. I have a dream that our people's understanding of the kingdom will include Dr. King's dream of a brotherhood and sisterhood that includes both sexes, all races, classes, church people and nonchurch people, that accepts all according to their gifts rather than their financial status or their place in society. I have a dream that we will be known as a caring community because we share our material possessions and are open to the poor, the divorced, the gay, the physically handicapped, the addicted.

I have a dream that our biblical discernment will help us wrestle with the hard questions, that we will tell our stories of faith and courage in difficult times. I have a dream that our awareness of the kingdom will extend to an active concern to reshape the political and economic structures of our local community; a concern that will be supportive of a world whose nations will share their resources without customs, duties, or other sanctions. I have a dream that our world will have immigration laws that will make us more mobile as a human family and able to respond quickly to famine and disasters of every kind. I have a dream that we will work together so well that the freedom to which God has called us will be the possession of every person, nation, and the international community, in a world where

The wolf lives with the lamb,
The panther lies down with the kid,
Calf and lion cub feed together. . . .
The cow and the bear make friends. . . .

                                      (Isaiah 11:6, JB)

My dream is the modern version of the dream of Jesus when he said, shortly after his baptism, "Repent, the kingdom of heaven is close at hand" (Matthew 4:17, JB). His "repent" is the ongoing call to conversion, to new possibilities in human life that approximate the ideal of the kingdom that will never be fully realized in this life.

What happened to the dreams of the fifties, sixties, and seventies? The flower children of Haight-Ashbury in San Francisco dreamed of a world in which there would be no more conflict, only love. The student movement under the leadership of Mario Salvo at Berkeley dreamed of a campus in which faculty and students would form a fraternity to replace a bureaucratic hierarchy. The quarter of a million people who listened to the dream speech of King at the Washington Monument dreamed that they themselves would make the dream a reality. The Vietnam protester dreamed of a world without war. During the euphoric days of Vatican II, Catholics believed that the church was on the edge of creating a kingdom to be fully realized during their lifetime. The true believers of the human potential movement believed that one more sensitivity workshop would rid them of their last hang-up and make them completely free. What will happen to the dream of the women in the modern feminist movement that is trying to liberate the church from its chauvinism and purge sexual discrimination from public life?

The dream will not be fulfilled until the Second Coming, when this world has passed away. This chapter is about how we meanwhile keep the dream alive and how we become purified rather than destroyed by our dreams. We must be alert to listen to the stories of the people who have internalized the dream, have been faithful to the dream—or who have even willingly surrendered to a violent death for the sake of the dream.

Dr. King's dream speech deepened his commitment to the dream that brought about his early death. In his last speech in Memphis the night before he died, he said,

> Like anybody I would like to live a long life. Longevity has its place. But I'm not concerned about that now. I just want to do God's will. And He's allowed me to go up to the mountain. And I've looked over, and I've seen the promised land. I may not get there with you, but I want you to know tonight that we as a people will get to the promised land. So I'm not worried about anything. I'm not fearing any man. "Mine eyes have seen the glory of the coming of the Lord."[2]

The next day he entered into glory.

The paradigm of faithfulness to the dream is found in Jesus and his relationship with his apostles. At his baptism he proclaimed the dream, then fleshed it out day by day with his stories and parables. When he made the decision to leave Galilee and face the consequences of his preaching in Jerusalem, he said he had to go there to suffer much and die.

In no way could they comprehend this foolishness, and they told him so. In his angry response Jesus called Peter a satan.

Even with this rebuke they could not grasp that he had to undergo suffering and a disgraceful death before he could come into glory.

As his disciples walked the Emmaus road after his resurrection and along the way shared their depression with a stranger, it finally in a flash came together at the inn as he broke bread with them. Their dream took flesh after this event as they day by day took up the cross and relived the death and rising modeled for them by Jesus. However, their conversion was in the moment of insight in the candlelight of the dining room. In the life of every Christian there are countless conversions, deaths and risings in both epic and ordinary events. In living the dream we become transformed. We ourselves become the gospel, the Good News. The dream leads us from Galilee to Jerusalem and back again to Galilee and up again to Jerusalem until we see the glory of the Lord.

While the dream opens us to the confusing and chaotic complexity of the world, it also starts us on a journey inward, into the wilderness of our interior life, where we meet the ravenous wild beasts and the ministering angels. We approach the journey inward with fear and reluctance. It is the place where we are most vulnerable. When our wraps are taken off, we stand frighteningly naked in a hall of mirrors. The accuser is not the racist, rapist, or warmonger, all of whom confirm us in our righteousness, but our selves who enter the hidden cavern with us and follow the trail that leads us to the burial place of the corpses we have hidden.

In ancient Greece, people walked fasting for days on a pilgrimage to the shrine of an oracle. When the pilgrims, tired and fasting, met the oracle, their deepest and most vulnerable emotions were on the surface. The oracle offered an ambiguous word to which they gave meaning that touched the deepest concerns in their lives. The pilgrims just listened to the inner stirrings that contained the answers to their questions. The oracle was the forerunner of the therapist who makes his living by saying "Aha."

The jail has always served this oracular function for the prophets. Eugene Debs, Dorothy Day, Martin Luther King, Jr., Anwar Sadat, and Malcolm X were gifted with prison sentences, as I have pointed out before. Ann Morrow Lindbergh in *Gift from the Sea* reflects as a woman of wealth and prestige who leaves her family to live in primitive conditions at the seashore, where she explores seashells that speak to her inner journey. The Ignatian Exercises and the Progoff meditations offer us guided tours to help us explore the darkness in our lives that threatens us in daylight.

Fire is an archetypal symbol of what happens in our dreams. *Quest for Fire* is the story of a primitive tribe that in a raid loses its prized possession of fire. The tribe then commissions three braves to steal fire from a neighboring tribe. The film relates their encounters with danger, suffering, and death in the process of successfully retrieving fire. The braves' capacity for survival is challenged by less developed tribes and by saber-toothed tigers and mastodons. However, in the course of their odyssey they meet a woman who teaches them how to make fire. After an arduous journey they return with the prized fire. In their joyous celebration of the event, the receptacle containing the fire falls into a swamp and is extinguished. But in the midst of the sudden shock, one of the braves reveals his new skill at making fire.[3]

When the magic that has kept the gleam in our eyes fails to excite us, the fire that has fueled our dream is extinguished. But our creativeness reaches its peak when the fire goes out and we must rely on our imagination. The fire that is kindled in the midst of darkness and despair has a new quality richer than the fire that fueled the original dream. We are again possessed by it and passionately live it again.

The prophet will continually experience the feeling of aloneness and what mystics like John of the Cross call the dark night of the soul and moderns refer to as burnout or depression. A spiritual life that has been cultivated by constant prayer will turn the depth of despair to a dynamism that is likened to fire. The Pentecostal fire is never far from the prophetic parish. When our feet falter, when our vision blurs and the dream seems to elude us, a spark will emerge, the fire will kindle, and parishioners will go forth with the new fire in their eyes.

Notes

Chapter 1

1. Thomas P. Sweetser, S.J., "The Parish as a Faith Community," *Chicago Studies,* Summer, 1979, p. 239. This study is a summary of "seven stories" of widely diverse parishes. The full development of the study is published in *Successful Parishes* (Minneapolis: Winston Press, 1983).

Chapter 3

1. Roger Mahony, "The Eucharist and Social Justice," *Worship,* January 1983, p. 60.
2. Dennis J. Geaney, O.S.A., "Keeping Things Together," *Orate Fratres,* January 1951, p. 49.
3. Donald Senior, C.P., *Jesus* (Dayton, Ohio: Pflaum, 1975), p. 47.
4. Juan Matteos, "The Jewish World at the Time of Jesus," *Sojourners,* July 1977, p. 19.

Chapter 4

1. Gregory Baum, "Blessed Are the Poor," *The Ecumenist,* October 1978, p. 1.
2. John A. Coleman, S.J., "The Social Encyclicals: Development of Church Social Teaching," *Origins* II, no. 3:33.
3. *To Campaign for Justice* (Washington, D.C.: United States Catholic Conference, 1982), p. 34.
4. *Excuse Me, America,* 16mm color film, 47 min. (San Francisco: Archdiocesan Communications Center of San Francisco, 1978).
5. John Roach at a press conference, bishops' meeting, November 1982.
6. *Gods of Metal,* 16mm color film, 27 min. (Maryknoll, N.Y.: Maryknoll Films, 1982).
7. Thomas Gumbleton, address at Holy Cross College, Worcester, Mass., April 10, 1983.

Chapter 5
1. Henri Nouwen, "The Parish: A Safe Place to Face Our Pain," *Celebration,* September 1981, p. 343.

Chapter 6
1. Joe Holland and Peter Henriot, S.J., *Social Analysis: Linking Faith and Justice* (Washington, D.C.: Center of Concern, 1980), p. 3.
2. Ibid.

Chapter 7
1. John A. Coleman, S.J., *An American Strategic Theology* (Ramsey, N.J.: Paulist, 1982), p. 46.
2. Parish bulletin of February 15, 1981, p. 2.

Chapter 8
1. George Schopp, *Upturn* (Journal of Association of Chicago Priests), March 1983, p. 2.
2. James Malone, "How Effective Is the Church's Social Doctrine?" *Origins,* November 26, 1981, p. 377.
3. Taken from *Empowerment by the Spirit* (Ramsey, N.J.: Paulist, 1981), p. 20.

Chapter 9
1. George F. Kennan, "Views," *Chicago Sun-Times,* November 28, 1982, sec. 2, p. 4.
2. Ibid., p. 5.

Chapter 10
1. Dolores Curran, *Women Moving Church* (Washington, D.C.: Center of Concern, 1982), p. 2.
2. Pat Mische, *Women Moving Church* (Washington, D.C.: Center of Concern, 1982), p. 3.
3. Sebastian Moore, *The Inner Loneliness* (New York: Crossroad, 1982), p. 83.
4. Julian, *Showings,* translated from the critical text with an introduction by Edmund Colledge and James Walsh; Preface by Jean Leclerq (Ramsey, N.J.: Paulist, 1978), p. 11.
5. Ibid., p. 9.

6. "Task Force Report on the Role of Women," *Catholic Herald* (Milwaukee), December 8, 1982, p. 4A.

Chapter 11

1. Abigail McCarthy, "World and Church Again," *Commonweal*, February 13, 1981, p. 73.
2. Robert N. Bellah, "Religion and Power in America Today," *Commonweal*, December 3, 1982, p. 655.
3. James Hennesey, S.J., *American Catholics* (New York: Oxford, 1981), p. 190.
4. "The Challenge of Peace: God's Promise and Our Response," *Origins* 13, no. 1 (May 13, 1983), pp. 2-3.
5. Andrew M. Greeley, "Selective Catholicism: How They Got Away With It," *America*, April 30, 1983, p. 336.
6. Gregory Baum, "Challenge to the Laity," *The Ecumenist*, May-June, 1981, p. 14.
7. Gregory Baum, *National Catholic Reporter*, September 3, 1982, p. 14.
8. John A. Coleman, S.J., "The Future of Ministry," *America*, March 28, 1981, p. 244.

Chapter 12

1. Jim Wallis, *The Call to Conversion* (San Francisco: Harper & Row, 1981).
2. James H. Forest, "Merton's Peacemaking," *Sojourners*, December 1979, p. 18.

Chapter 13

1. Martin Luther King, Jr., in his famous speech at Washington, D.C., in 1963. See "He Had a Dream," *Chicago Sun-Times*, Special Supplement, April 2, 1968, p. 3.
2. William Robert Martin, *Martin Luther King, Jr.* (New York: Waybright and Tally, 1968), p. 275.
3. John Harrington, "Interiority and Loss of Soul," *Chicago Studies*, Summer 1982.